DISCARD

Contemporary Canadian Painting

Contemporary Canadian Painting

William Withrow

McCLELLAND AND STEWART LIMITED/TORONTO

As with any project of this sort, I had
the help of a great many people.
Among them, I would like to thank
all the art dealers and the artists, with
whom I had many discussions and
consultations. Anita Aarons supplied
much of the research material and
Mrs. Grace Pincoe provided the
bibliographies. My secretary, Judy
Burke, was especially helpful. And my
wife, June, was ready with typing,
patience and understanding. I am
grateful to them all.

0-7710-9029-3

The Canadian Publishers
McClelland and Stewart Limited
Illustrated Book Division
25 Hollinger Road, Toronto 374

CONTENTS

This book deals with the work of twenty-four contemporary Canadian painters – "contemporary" in this case meaning active in the period since 1945.

Obviously twenty-four is no magic number. It is, in fact, a quite arbitrary figure and one that rules out a great number of excellent and even important Canadian painters. My criteria, admittedly subjective, were (a) quality (b) a persistent and unique visual image or (c) a catalytic function. In some cases all three factors were, to my mind, operative, in most at least two; and in defence of the selection I can only say that I have been looking at, thinking about and reacting to Canadian painting throughout these years. The choice was not easy.

But if the number of painters represented has no special intrinsic significance, the period being dealt with has. The quarter-century from 1945 to 1970 saw radical changes in the state of art and the artist in this country.

For one thing, it was the period when Canadian art finally caught up with the twentieth century. After all, abstract art was firmly established in Europe by the start of the *First* World War. Picasso, Matisse and Braque were deep into their explorations of the proposition that specifically artistic values resided in forms and colours, entirely independent of subject matter. Cubism had already made its official debut in 1907, in an exhibition in Paris. Wassily Kandinsky had painted his first completely non-representational work in Munich in 1910. Tachisme (action painting) had been tried, and Dada was on the way.

But in Canada – except for the lonely experiments of Bertram Brooker in the mid-twenties – the *Second* World War was over before abstract art was anything much more than a rumour.

Canada was an artistic backwater. A few fine, dedicated painters, such as Emily Carr and David Milne, struggled in poverty to express a singular vision, but otherwise Canadian artists were no more than competent provincials working in various academic traditions that were already at least thirty years out of date. Small wonder, at that, in a country where the art-nouveau landscapes of the Group of Seven were still considered avant-garde, and where the highest critical praise was reserved for "that peculiar combination of directness, sober restraint, honest expression and decorative intent that has made Canadian art what it is."

But, starting in the forties (in Montreal) and the early fifties (in Toronto), Canadian art finally joined the mainstream. In retrospect, the change was dramatically sudden: almost overnight, it seems. For example, the first Biennial of Canadian Painting was staged by the National Gallery in 1955 and was dominated by traditional figurative painting. The second, only two years later, was more than sixty per cent abstract. In less than two decades from the end of the Second World War, Canadian painting was overwhelmingly non-figurative, and a few non-figurative Canadian painters were even established firmly on the international scene. Jean-Paul Riopelle was the darling of Paris, and William Ronald was selling his total output in New York. (In 1956, Ronald had won a Guggenheim Award against international competition. In 1958, Jack Shadbolt of Vancouver won the same award, and the 1960 winner was Paul-Emile Borduas.) In 1971, Jack Bush was being called, by an American critic, "one of the important non-figurative artists painting today."

During the same period, and under the same stimulus of fresh ideas and larger ambitions, living artists became much more *visible* in Canada. There was an odd but definite effect of the number of Canadian painters having multiplied. This was unverifiable, since painting has not been a job occupation acknowledged by Statistics Canada, but certainly in place of a lone remembered Group of Seven, there were suddenly Painters Eleven and the Regina Five, not to mention Les Automatistes and Les Plasticiens in Montreal, and a "West Coast school." The sense of increased artistic activity was reinforced by the appearance of work by living Canadian artists not only in galleries and in the sedate annual society shows but in such unlikely public places as dealers' show-windows, airports, corporate foyers, city halls, and the sides of buildings in downtown Toronto. Furthermore, the work itself often became the subject of healthy – if sometimes jeering and contumacious – comment. During the period, there were debates, letters-to-the-editor, manifestos, protests and a court case about contemporary Canadian paintings. Art made news.

So did artists. They appeared on television, ran radio programs, were profiled in newspapers and popular magazines and even made the Canadian edition of *Time*. This was all part of another change that the same quarter-century witnessed: the change in the artist's status. It is not particularly an economic change. Though the most successful artists can live in substantial homes, travel at will and indulge expensive tastes of one sort or another (such as Riopelle's taste for fast sport cars), most of the rest are, as always, in no position to make a living painting full-time. Things haven't changed *that* much. Still, the artist in Canada does at last show signs of infiltrating the middle-class. If he depends for his income on teaching, he is no longer cast in the déclassé role of drawing-master, probably somewhere in the public school system. Instead, he is much more apt to be teaching at university level: a professor or, even more glamorously, an "artist-in-residence." And a Canadian artist is at last a plausible candidate not only for an honorary degree but for a medal from his country. The story of the years 1945-1970 is thus the story of art in Canada's coming of age, beginning at last to be accepted as a vital and meaningful element in Canadian society.

It is also the story of the end of an epoch. This book is strictly about painting. As such, it is probably the last book pretending to deal with art in Canada that can restrict itself with any validity only to those works involving the application of colour to a flat surface. Until recently, painting completely dominated the visual arts in this country. To refer to "an artist" was to mean "an easel-painter." If the twenty-four painters in this book had not existed, or had made their living stock-broking, there would have been almost literally no Canadian art to speak of in the fifteen years immediately following the Second World War. But, in the last few years, this has changed dramatically. These days, almost all the important artists in the country are experimenting with other forms and other means of expression. Indeed, an artist who still paints is regarded with disdain in some circles. If art is defined as aesthetic experience, today's artist perceives his role as achieving the experience by any legitimate means, and his function as problem-solving rather than object-making. Starting with "happenings," art as idea (generally called Conceptual Art) has captured the attention of some. So-called Electrical Art, Kinetic Art and Constructivism have attracted others. Still others have turned to poetry, photography, sound or multi-media creation. And, even before Expo 67 drew public attention to it as *the* art of the second half of the twentieth century, a number of Canadian painters had left their easels to work in film – some of them, such as Michael Snow and Joyce Wieland, to make their names abroad as film-makers rather than as painters. That is why Snow and Wieland are represented in this book with no work later than 1964. Of the twenty-four artists here dealt with, more than a third have abandoned painting altogether in the last four or five years, or have demoted it to second or third place in their hierarchy of creative activities. As a footnote to the end of an era: only six of the twenty-four still use an easel at all.

A period that has brought such a quickening in the country's art cannot be chronicled easily.

People – individuals – made some of the difference: displaced painters from war-torn Europe bringing news of the latest fashions in art; a handful of inspired teachers at home, pariahs as like as not in the Establishment art schools; here and there a crucial, imaginative gallery director/commercial dealer/civil servant/collector/patron. The painters themselves, of course: their stories are worth knowing about.

Conditions made a difference, too: social and economic change, affluence, the rise of radicalism. Some institutions and associations played a part, and so, most importantly, did communications, including television and even the popular magazines. In the global village, art cannot remain old-fashioned and parochial forever. But if it is true that "creation comes from an overflow," perhaps it is simply that Canada at least had energy to spare for the arts that older cultures take for granted.

Some say the beginnings of change should be dated from 1940, when Alfred Pellan, who had been painting in Paris until the Nazi invasion, came home to Montreal with his baggage full of his own audacious avant-garde work and his head full of the newest European trends and theories. Some would put it even earlier, and some would put it later: the date most often mentioned is 1948, marked by the publication in Montreal of the controversial manifesto, *Refus Global*.

But the year the Second World War ended in Europe is as apt a starting point for the story as any, for two reasons. The first is that Emily Carr died in 1945. In her isolated, desperate struggle to express herself, and to survive as an artist in Canada, she stands as a symbol of what it was like in the first half of this century. The prejudice against the artist was almost complete. No middle class family was less than dismayed if a child determined to be a painter. As a result the enrolment in art schools came strikingly from the lower classes, with a scattering of dilettante debutantes and a few aristocrats in rebellion. The art schools themselves were hidebound and conservative, dedicated to drawing from life and copying from reproductions of the old masters. Technique was everything; experiment, and particularly "modernism," was firmly quelled. The art societies, in their pursuit of an aura of Establishment respectability, were not much more daring.

Scarcely a painter, of whatever degree of safe competency, could make a living from his "fine" art alone. The idea seemed to be to postpone buying the work of a Canadian artist until he was safely dead and his reputation reliably established. As A. Y. Jackson, in *A Painter's Country*, has said, "Painting in Canada has always been a precarious way of making a living. Only the poets rank lower than the artists in the financial scale." As for any "modernistic" painter, he could scarcely get exhibition space, let alone a one-man show or a commercial dealer to handle his work. (There were, of course, very few dealers and an extremely restricted market. As late as 1950, only five commercial galleries were advertising in the Montreal *Star*; there are now forty-four.) He settled, when he could get it, for exhibiting along with amateurs, and near-amateurs, or in department stores, hotel lobbies and restaurants. Harold Town, who was graduated from the Ontario College of Art in 1944, had to wait until 1953 to sell his first abstract painting (for a hundred and fifty dollars), and until *1954* for his first one-man gallery show. The foreword to an exhibition catalogue from the forties of the Contemporary Arts Society (founded by Montreal artist John Lyman in 1939 and named with hopeful impressiveness) is revealingly plaintive: "The object of the CAS is to bring you the modern art of our time. . . . Enterprise of this sort is one function of the CAS but it has another equally important – to awaken interest in our own Canadian tradition, which cannot thrive without moral and material support from the community."

And yet, terribly belatedly, and just before her death, Emily Carr had been recognized by the then-official art world of Canada, in the person of the National Gallery director, Eric Brown. That, too, was a symbol. For, at war's end, events *were* stirring in this country. Something *was* afoot.

It was in 1945 that a group from the Arts and Letters Club (a luncheon club in Toronto made famous by the membership of the Group of Seven) began pushing actively for government support for Canadian culture. From this small germinal endeavour sprouted such ramifications as to alter significantly the situation of the arts in Canada. The first step was the organization of the Canadian Arts Council, representing sixteen national cultural enterprises. (Later, in 1959, it became the

Canadian Conference of the Arts.) Through the efforts of this council, Prime Minister Mackenzie King's government agreed to set up a Royal Commission (how Canadian!) to investigate the National Development in the Arts, Letters and Sciences. The commission chairman was the Right Honourable Vincent Massey and its report, known as the Massey Report, was published in 1951. The Massey Report led directly to the establishment in 1957 of the Canada Council.

But the flowering of contemporary Canadian painting is a complex phenomenon, and long before that landmark event all sorts of other things had happened.

They happened first in Montreal. When Alfred Pellan returned from Paris it had been possible for some years, thanks to the efforts of a few Montreal dealers, for Quebec artists to see examples of the work of such members of the Paris school as Redon and Modigliani. Almost before Pellan's first Canadian exhibition was over, he was attracting students and experimenting with fresh techniques. Meanwhile the Montreal artist-teacher Paul-Emile Borduas had been struggling to free himself from the simultaneous inhibitions of a clergy-ridden Quebec and of traditional representational painting. In official art circles, resistance to non-figurative art was strong, but in 1942 Borduas began painting his first abstracts, using a sort of automatic, action-painting approach. He soon had a group of disciples, Les Automatistes, with whom he exhibited, and it was this group, along with other like-minded young radicals, that in 1948 published the collection of rebellious plays and essays called *Refus Global*. The title was taken from the introductory essay, written by Borduas himself. It was not a document of aesthetic theory but of political and social protest. Borduas was strongly critical of the repressive forces of organized religion: "To hell with the incense-burners and holy-wine sippers!" He called also for an end to the suffocating political and social atmosphere of "Duplessis' Quebec." (The group, including Pierre Trudeau, that was publishing *Cité Libre* at about the same time shared the same concerns but was suspicious of Borduas-style emotional idealism and in contrast stressed the intellect.) The publication of *Refus Global* caused a furor. Borduas was fired from his job as instructor at L'Ecole du Meuble and thus became a martyr and a hero. And somehow the episode was a magically liberating force for young Quebec painters. When Les Automatistes waned in influence in 1954, their place was quickly taken by Les Plasticiens: four young Montreal artists (Louis Belzile, Fernand Toupin, Jean-Paul Jérome and "Jauran," pseudonym of art critic Rodolphe de Repentigny) who had been exhibiting together and who in 1955 issued a manifesto. French-Canadian artists differ from their English-speaking colleagues in one main respect: their love of manifestos. The inspiration for Les Plasticiens was mainly Piet Mondrian and their aim was to purify art by emphasizing the formal elements. Two artists who appear in this book, Guido Molinari and Claude Tousignant, though never members of Les Plasticiens, had very similar aims and, with others, formed a second plasticien group about the time the first one was breaking up. The important difference between the first group and the second was the change in orientation: away from the European tradition and towards New York. The most important post-war development in international art had been the evolution of the so-called New York School and the consequent shifting of the art world's focus from Paris to America. This new generation of Quebec painters had been quick to recognize the shift. The Quebec art scene remains a vigorous and experimental one, which seems only fitting since it is generally agreed that twentieth-century Canadian painting was born there in 1948.

Toronto was slower off the mark. (Ottawa was slower still: in Canada's first appearance at the Venice Biennale in 1952, the powers-that-were chose to represent current Canadian art with Emily Carr, David Milne, Goodridge Roberts and Alfred Pellan.) 1948 was the year that the Womens' Committee of the Art Gallery of Toronto held its first exhibition and sale of contemporary Canadian paintings. Since commercial outlets for living artists were almost non-existent at the time, several Toronto dealers claim that these sales (which were annual events for a decade or more) laid the groundwork for the subsequent lively art market in Toronto.

But it was groundwork only. As in Montreal, the embattled non-figurative artists took the most important step. A group of them had been quietly assembling themselves—so quietly, in fact, as to be almost in secret. They scarcely knew each other or each others' work. But in 1953 William Ronald, who was doing some commercial design work for the Robert Simpson Company, talked his employers into building a home-decoration promotion around abstract art. Called *Abstracts at Home,* the show featured the paintings of seven local artists, including Ronald, as motifs for room settings. The seven participating artists began discussing the possibility of gaining impact by other joint exhibitions and in due course, along with four other artists, formed Painters Eleven. Their first exhibition, held at the Roberts Gallery, February 12 to 28, 1954, consisted of thirty-three works by Jack Bush, Jock Macdonald, Harold Town, William Ronald, Kazuo Nakamura, Tom Hodgson, Oscar Cahen, Alexandra Luke, Roy Mead, Walter Yarwood and Hortense Gordon. Though few paintings were sold (and though the Roberts Gallery proved singularly uninterested in adding any of the painters to its stable), the show drew the largest crowds in the gallery's history. The crowds may well have been somewhat baffled by the group's statement in the show catalogue, which read in part, "There is no manifesto here for the times. There is no jury but time. By now there is little harmony in the noticeable disagreement. But there is profound regard for the consequences of our complete freedom." Still, it is interesting to compare the last sentence with one in Borduas' *Refus Global*: "au refus global nous opposons la responsabilité entière."

During the next five years Painters Eleven exhibited regularly together, as well as separately. In 1956 they exhibited as a group at the annual American Abstract Painters Exhibition in New York, to so favourable a press that their own compatriots were at last impressed. In 1957 they were invited to contribute the "maiden show" of the important new Park Gallery in Toronto. And in 1958 the Quebec artist, Jacques de Tonnancour, arranged for the group to have a show at L'Ecole des Beaux Arts in Montreal. Up to that time there had been no active co-operation between the revolutionary artists in the two cities but now Robert Ayre, the respected art critic of the Montreal *Star*, wrote, "The Eleven are sensational painters, for the most part working on a bigger scale than the Quebec non-objectives and with much greater violence." The *next year*, Painters Eleven formally disbanded. Their work of forcing public recognition and acceptance of abstract art was, they felt, done.

It had been, in so short a time, a formidable accomplishment. One factor had been the opening in Toronto of one or two new commercial galleries sympathetic to abstract art. Hitherto only the Picture Loan Society gallery, operated by that delightfully aristocratic benefactor of Canadian art, Douglas Duncan, had given house room to avant-garde young artists. But in 1955 it was joined by what is now the Isaacs Gallery and, shortly, by Barry Kernerman's Gallery of Contemporary Art. The GCA failed after three years, but not before making a contribution to the public climate of acceptance for the new art.

A contribution to change on a wider scale was the appointment, also in 1955, of a new director for the National Gallery, Alan Jarvis. Dr. Jarvis, a Canadian, a Rhodes scholar and a practising sculptor, had great sympathy for living Canadian artists and in his first year as director not only purchased the work of twenty-six Canadians for the Gallery but undertook a cross-country tour during which he made 158 speeches promoting contemporary art and the National Gallery.

Almost as though it were springing up in his wake, the artistic flowering that had begun in

Montreal in the forties and sprouted in Toronto in the early fifties, now appeared in the west. In the late fifties the focus shifted from the two older art centres to one of the most unlikely locations in Canada: Regina, Saskatchewan. Not that Regina had totally lacked for artists; in fact, early in the thirties, one of the province's first serious artists, an Englishman named A. F. Kenderdine, had founded an art camp at Murray Point, Emma Lake, north of Prince Albert. In the fifties this camp became the summer school of the University of Saskatchewan's art school. The faculty of the school, perhaps feeling the need for outside inspiration themselves, wisely began adding to the regular six-week session a two-week seminar for practising artists, conducted by a series of guest lecturers. The guests were leading American painters, critics and even composers. The two who seem to have had the greatest impact were the late Barnett Newman, an important colour-field painter from New York, and art critic Clement Greenberg, also from New York and undoubtedly the most influential exponent of colour-field painting, or, as it was later called in an exhibition mounted to feature this type of work, Post-Painterly Abstraction. Newman — who was invited by Ron Bloore, then director of the Norman Mackenzie Art Gallery of the University of Saskatchewan, and by two instructors of the art department on the same campus, Roy Kiyooka and Arthur McKay — came in 1959. Newman brought none of his work with him, and did no painting while there, but his personality and convictions seem to have fired the Emma Lake Workshop participants with new and more serious ambitions. In 1961, Bloore was able to organize an exhibition called *Five Painters from Regina* that proved so important and interesting that the National Gallery reorganized it and circulated it across the country.

Greenberg came to Regina in the summer of 1962. Bloore, a moving spirit in the seminars, was on a sabbatical in Greece and when he returned he was profoundly disturbed to find most of his artist colleagues "converted" to colour-field painting. Greenberg certainly did not invent the Regina School, as persistent myth would have it, but he did have a profound effect.

At almost the same time as the Regina phenomenon, Vancouver also earned the attention of the Canadian art world. The activity centred around the Vancouver School of Art, where artist-teacher Bert Binning was producing cubistic abstractions in the early fifties. But it was Jack Shadbolt whose powerful personality and effective leadership as a teacher and painter provided the main impetus to the coastal art awakening. The art community there was not, by the way, as isolated as easterners are wont to believe. They were aware of the lively work being done by artists in Seattle and San Francisco and both paintings and people travelled back and forth, then as now, on a north-south axis. But Roy Kiyooka arrived in 1959 with his ambitious, New York-oriented work, and through it and the stimulus of his guru presence broke down the barriers that had tended to separate the British Columbian artists from the main stream. From that time to the present Vancouver has been given equal status with Montreal and Toronto/London as a major centre of creative activity, consistently producing work of international interest.

This scene has been aided by the vigorous and imaginative management of the Vancouver Art Gallery, with its almost exclusive commitment to the art of today, and by the program of the Fine Arts Gallery of the University of British Columbia, where exhibitions of the most experimental art by known and unknown young local artists have been given serious treatment. Commercial galleries find it difficult to survive economically in Vancouver, but the Douglas Gallery, in co-operation with galleries in New York and Los Angeles, has made a contribution by showing first-quality American contemporary art, thus further de-regionalizing the Vancouver art scene.

These days, in the view of many, one of the greatest contributions to West Coast development in the visual arts is being made through Intermedia — a loosely organized group of some sixty artists who got together in 1967 to form a vehicle for co-operative ventures in related arts; for example, the combination of the visual arts with poetry, dance and music. Freer in concept than Experiments in Art and Technology (an international movement with branches in Canada that began about the same time), Intermedia has not limited its endeavours to technologically-orientated art. Not only has it contributed to the widening of intellectual and aesthetic horizons for both participants and audiences, it has stood for a rarity in the arts, creative co-operation.

If Regina as a centre for innovative artists seemed unlikely in the early sixties, London, Ontario, perhaps the most conservative small city in Canada, seemed unthinkable. But, in the mid-sixties, this is what happened. With the return of Jack Chambers and Greg Curnoe to their home town, a quiet artistic revolution began, which soon became noisy enough and exciting enough to dominate the consciousness of the whole Canadian art world.

Curnoe and Chambers were joined after 1965 by a lively group of young artists, including John Boyle, Murray Favro, Bev Kelly, Ron Martin, David and Royden Rabinowitch, Walter Redinger, Edward Zelenak and Tony Urquhart. Half had studied locally at Beal Technical School and therefore knew each other, and this creative group grew to include poets, photographers and film-makers, so that an unself-conscious cross-pollination stimulated the imaginations of all. Multimedia, collaborative efforts evolved, such as the publication of *Region Magazine* and *20 Cent Magazine*, and the establishment of an artists' co-op gallery. In a spirit of playfulness, the artists also formed the Canadian Nihilist Party, devoted mainly to organizing parties and to the holding of an annual "family" picnic. The Nihilist Spasm Band, a now-famous band made up of artists playing their own homemade instruments, contributed to the relaxed, apolitical chaos. This atmosphere is cleverly captured in a comic-book-style catalogue which accompanied the National Gallery exhibition of London artists' work, called *The Heart of London,* in 1968. All agreed that London in the sixties was an inhospitable climate for creative people and they inevitably drew together "against" the conservative Establishment, in which they included, rather unfairly, the London Public Library and Art Museum. There was, though, one moment of sympathetic rapport between the artists and the London gallery. This came at the time of the gallery's nostalgic ethnic-object show, called *Cultural Heritage of This Region.* The artists themselves were regionally oriented and this show struck such a responsive chord in them that on closing night they gathered to read their own poetry within the display galleries. The year was 1967, centennial year.

Psychologically at least, centennial year and Expo 67 were the climax of the post-war artistic awakening in Canada. The drama had gained momentum all through the sixties.

First there was the Great Art Boom. Its centre was Toronto, since Toronto was where the money was, and it was detected and labelled by the media at the start of the sixties mainly as the result of Harold Town's extraordinary near-sellout show at The Laing Gallery in 1961. Actually, it had been building for two or three years, as the industry's dollar volume quintupled and the market share of non-figurative art, on a pictures-sold basis, jumped from about ten per cent to somewhere near eighty-five per cent. Collectors, it seemed, had begun to buy Canadian abstract art in wholesale lots. Certainly Mr. and Mrs. Samuel J. Zacks, Toronto's most important art collectors (though hitherto only of European art) had bought eighteen Canadian works in a single Sunday afternoon and had then brought the total up to seventy in a whirlwind cross-country tour. Artists' prices began doubling and even tripling, and at the same time commercial galleries began to multiply—and flourish. Avrom Isaacs moved to a spacious new gallery on Yonge Street near Yorkville, where he soon had Dorothy Cameron's gallery as a neighbour. Miss Cameron's gallery came to stress sculpture and prints, and eventually closed—for the record—not because of a court case over a show which was supposed to have been obscene (whatever that means) but because the exuberant director oversubsidized her operation into the red. The adventurous Carman Lamana Gallery now occupies this space. The Jerrold Morris Gallery first located in glamorous quarters in a Bloor Street skyscraper, though it soon had to reopen in more modest form in an old house one block north. Thus it joined Gallery Moos in a new concentration of serious art galleries which soon included the Dunkelman Gallery, Albert White and Nancy Poole (formerly of London, Ontario) and three or four others.

It certainly looked like a boom. Suddenly, too — as if someone were trying to make up overnight for years of neglect — no fewer than three exhibitions of contemporary Canadian art were mounted at the Commonwealth Institute in London, England.

What's more, in the very same year the Department of Transport initiated its ambitious program of art for the airports of Canada. This project fortunately came under the bold leadership of J. R. Baldwin, Deputy Minister of the Department, who had been encouraged to follow the European example of providing a percentage, generally two per cent, for works of art in all new government buildings. John C. Parkin of Toronto, art patron and head of the architectural firm that had been commissioned to create the new International Airport at Toronto, was one of the most persuasive voices in promoting the two per cent idea. Baldwin won the support of Cabinet Ministers Leon Balcer and George Hees for this history-making expenditure on art from the Diefenbaker Government. But, with typical Canadian caution, the Government was prepared to approve only one-half of one per cent. This was applied to the new airports at Toronto, Winnipeg, Edmonton and Vancouver. (Montreal had already been built.) Nonetheless, it was a great coup.

The artists were chosen by excellent juries across the country and were well paid. They were also encouraged to visit sites at least twice. In spite of this, about half the commissions turned out to be less than satisfactory or, in a few unfortunate cases, disastrous. But if the results were less than hoped for, the injection of half a million dollars into the pockets of Canadian artists through the program was an unassailable Good. And a few, such as Jack Shadbolt's mural in Edmonton and Brian Fisher's in Montreal, work very well, presenting Canadian art to both national and international visitors in a highly effective and uncontrived way. Artists in this book who received commissions for the art-in-airports projects include Alfred Pellan (Winnipeg), Jack Shadbolt (Edmonton), Jean-Paul Riopelle (Toronto) and Harold Town (Toronto).

It was during the sixties, too, that the Canada Council at last paid off for artists. Established in 1957, the early activities of the Council had been heavily weighted in favour of the more vociferously needy performing arts. Prior to its existence, a few artists had received Canadian Government Overseas Awards, arrangements worked out with France and Italy after the Second World War, through which war-debt money could be used by Canadians studying in those countries. Most of the beneficiaries of the $6,000-a-year awards were scholars; artists for the most part did not even know of their availability. And similar ignorance persisted after the establishment of the Canada Council. This changed when David Silcox, former undergraduate secretary of Hart House, University of Toronto (and, as such, the curator of the Hart House Art Collection), joined the Council staff as Visual Arts Officer. This is not to say that the management of the Council prior to Silcox's appointment had been hostile to the visual arts: it simply had required someone to publicize the existence of the Council to Canadian painters and sculptors. This meant travel. In 1966, Silcox instigated a travelling jury system. Silcox feels that the choice of this first jury was a considerable factor in establishing the artists' confidence in the work of the Council. The first jurors were painter Ron Bloore, printmaker Albert Dumouchel, and art critic Elizabeth

Kilbourn. They travelled across the country, coast to coast, talking to artists and looking at their work. This innovative field-work was eventually copied by the other arts divisions within the Council. Before this time it had all been done by mail.

Silcox was also responsible for some other policy departures. He directed money for the first time to art museums – initially for special projects and for fifty-fifty help with art purchases, and later for straight operating costs. This had hitherto been done only for performing-arts companies: the Council, unaware of the heavy costs of mounting exhibitions and conducting educational programs, apparently had the idea that museums needed only to pay their light and heat and keep their doors open. Silcox also arranged short-term grants to artists for special projects: material grants to cover the outlay for a show, or modest travel grants to permit attendance at their own out-of-town openings or simple visits to other Canadian cities. Until the mid-sixties, few artists in Canada had had an opportunity to meet each other, let alone to gather nationally. Silcox invented a series of meetings, called *Soundings,* paid for by the Council. The first one was held in Montreal in 1966. It was not only the first time that artists from across the country had been brought together to talk about mutual problems but the first time they had had a chance to talk to Government, with the assurance that Government was listening.

At the beginning of the sixties, less than twenty-five per cent of the moneys from the Council went to the visual arts. By the end of the decade the ratio was approaching forty-five per cent.

The excitement and achievement of the sixties reached its peak in centennial year. The national consciousness, the new sense of national identity and purpose with which Canada had emerged from the Second World War, had been growing quietly, steadily. Now it exploded in joyous celebration. And, for the first time, the Canadian public visibly shared the excitement and pride in their nation's creative achievement that had thitherto seemed the private experience of only a few professionals and collectors.

And yet . . . Canadian sculptors were generously patronized and their works, commissioned for the most part by the Canadian Corporation for the 1967 World Exhibition, dotted the Expo grounds. Architecture and film fared brilliantly well. But painting played only a minor role. Canadian painting was limited to a modest exhibition displayed in the entrance foyer of the Canadian Government pavilion. Organized by Barry Lord, it was called *Painting in Canada.* (Of the forty-four artists, twenty are represented in this book.) The most important art exhibition at Expo was *Man and His World,* a selection of international art covering the full range of art history down through the ages. It included two Canadian paintings, one by Paul-Emile Borduas and one by Jean-Paul Riopelle.

From the perspective of 1972 it is possible to see that centennial year was not just a climax but another turning-point in the history of Canadian art.

The Great Art Boom, of course, turned out to be, in the words of Robert Fulford in the Toronto *Star,* "the art boom that never really happened." Less than a year after Expo, Canada experienced a serious economic recession. Dealers began to admit privately that sales of Canadian art had almost dried up. Some commercial galleries had to close down, including that of Dorothy Cameron, who had sold half a million dollars' worth of Canadian art in only six years. Far from appreciating in value, some paintings first sold in the fifties were knocked down at auction for less than the original price. Only the gilt-edged Canadian painters – the Group of Seven, David Milne, Paul-Emile Borduas – have held firm in the market. What happened? The main fact that escaped the art journalists during the golden years was the real size of the market. Those who cared enough to buy numbered only a few hundred. When their walls were full, the good times were over. Art museums, of course, could not sustain the boom, for in many cases their purchase funds are donated by the same collectors.

At the same time costs were rising sharply. In 1960, it was possible to open a gallery in Toronto on sixty dollars a month for operating costs. By 1970, monthly expenses for many Toronto galleries were running as high as $3,000. Though the average price-tag on a painting had risen in the same decade from $125 to $2,000, survival had become a hand-to-mouth affair. Painters, who in 1967 had looked forward to making a living from their art, were back to teaching and driving taxicabs in the established Canadian artistic tradition.

And yet art is more than ever alive and well and living in Canada. I offer in evidence:

Item: The fact that Toronto continues as the commercial art centre of Canada and one of the major centres for contemporary art in North America was underlined by the recent move of Montreal's leading dealer, Mira Godard, to Toronto. Miss Godard, in alliance with the powerful international Marlborough galleries, opened a handsome establishment in Yorkville "village." The Godard-Lefort gallery will still continue in Montreal but the implication of the move is clear. As one of my French-Canadian artist friends says, "Québec libre, hell! Québec broke! Without my Ontario market I couldn't survive." Artists are great survivors.

Item: With the coming to London, Ontario, of certain more internationally-minded artists, and the development of a non-Canadian staff in the art department of the new Fanshawe College of Applied Arts and Technology in nearby Welland, Greg Curnoe and a few of his closer friends added to their regional philosophy an intense nationalism. But, by 1969, many of the London group had also become politicized in another sense. In line with the long-established concern of Jack Chambers for "artist's rights," the London group became the national headquarters for an artist's union: c.a.r. (Canadian Artists Representation). This organization is currently pressing the art museums of Canada for rental fees for exhibiting and other "fair exchange" practices, including copyright remuneration for the reproduction of their works. To my mind, many of their demands are not only justified but long overdue. Unfortunately, justice and economics come into conflict in this matter with the result that smaller art museums cannot face the budget implications of the artists' demands. In fact, they will be able to exhibit international contemporary art for less! In spite of the unrealistic nature of the fee schedule, especially as it applies to smaller centres, most Canadian art museum directors wish the now 250-member organization well, as generally cordial negotiations proceed toward mutual workable agreements between artists and museums.

Item: No living artist in this book has stopped contributing, in one way or another, to the sum of our collective aesthetic experience. Some, such as Jack Bush, are painting better than ever, reaching new heights. (For those who still care most about painting: young artists coming up include a reassuring number who apparently want to paint on canvas in a more or less traditional manner.) Some, such as Wieland and Snow, are blazing important trails in other, related, fields. And, what's more, the new technology embraced by the artists is being matched by a public acceptance of new forms and aesthetic modes. Something *has* changed in Canada in this quarter-century.

There is one more question to be considered. As illustrations for this book were being gathered, it crossed my mind that the title might be more accurately *Painting in Canada*. It is about artists who live and work in Canada and, in all but three cases, who were born here. They all came to artistic maturity in this country and presumably absorbed something of the Canadian environment in the process. That there is a peculiarly Canadian environment, or Canadian "experience" if you wish, even the internationalists and continentalists will not deny. Life in Canada is (still) different from anywhere else. Only in Russia, for example, could one experience the same feeling/ knowledge of our vast and rugged topography combined with our northernness and consequently harsh climate. But the Russian experience is eastern while ours is western and "new world." For, while most of our land is raw and undeveloped, we are nevertheless a highly-developed, techno- logical, western nation. At the same moment that we enjoy the sophisticated pleasures of our urban centres, we are troubled by the knowledge of our great and underpopulated northland. The very fact that we are seeking our identity with hitherto unheard-of intensity as though we were an "emerging nation" must of itself make the Canadian experience unique.

And so, in this document of the post-war artistic quickening in Canada, it is tempting to look for the "Canadianism" in Canadian painting.

Our Canadian identity is certainly strongly manifest in many of our contemporary arts: in the novels of Marie-Claire Blais and Margaret Laurence, for example, or in the poetry of Irving Layton, or in that especially insistent voice of our identity crisis, Gaston Miron, or in Canadian films like *Mon Oncle Antoine* by Claude Jutra, or *The Best Damn Fiddler From Calabogie to Kaladar* by Peter Pearson.

But, so far as I can see, it is not there in contemporary Canadian painting. If I were to enter a room filled with artists from many nations, including the twenty-four Canadians in this book, I feel sure that I could pick them out of the crowd (given that their appearance was completely unknown to me); but if I was faced with the same challenge in terms of their paintings in an exhibition of international contemporary art, I know my score would be low indeed. To me, at least, the nationality is simply not there: not that *"presence of the horizon"* that one critic has claimed to detect; not that "curious stylelessness (Canadians are Unique in being immensely civilized but relatively uncultured)" perceived by another critic; certainly not "that peculiar combination of directness, sober restraint, honest expression and decorative intent" praised in Canadian art by a third. The paintings illustrated in this book are, to me, both individual to their creators and international in their approach. It is significant that the two Canadian artists represented here who are most self-consciously Canadian, Joyce Wieland and Greg Curnoe, work in styles that have their roots in international pop art, so that both artists have to resort to using words in their work to convey their specifically national messages. But then universality is the very essence of an abstract art. And in any case that is perhaps the best way for it to be.

Through the ages, art has been employed in the service of many ideas; magic, religion, politics — and nationalism. Nationalism is the sum of a way of thinking and feeling, a relationship of people with a particular geographic and political entity. If one accepts this definition, one has to accept the fact that nationalism is difficult to translate into visual terms. But at one stage in the Canadian experience, the art of the Group of Seven served our image of ourselves very well.

Now our collective experience has out-stripped that art. If, in turn, our art has gone beyond any current definition of nationalism, perhaps it is only that our art is more mature than our politics. At any rate, it has lost its early innocence.

Yet, in spite of this, there *is* a kind of nationalism in Canadian painting. A non-objective painting by Borduas is Canadian — not because anyone other than a knowledgeable critic could recognize it as such. That doesn't matter. What matters is that as a Canadian I *know* it was painted by a Canadian: I know that such a Canadian painting exists. It enters into my feelings about Canada that I know it is a country that has painters.

That is why this book is dedicated to them.   WILLIAM WITHROW

J.W.G. Macdonald

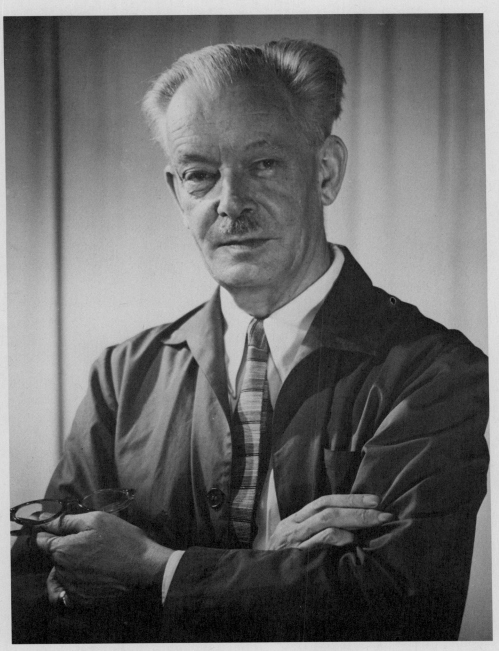

I move as I move consciously in relation to my awareness of nature. I do not see how I can work otherwise and be true to myself. I must be true to myself or else I cease to be a creative artist. Apart from my own efforts in the field of art my greatest happiness is in the odd favourable opportunities I have to fight for the worthiness I sense in the work of younger artists....

Midway through the period 1945-72, Canada had lost two of her most important artist-teachers, J. W. G. "Jock" Macdonald and Paul-Emile Borduas (pages 25-32). By age they belonged to the generation of Canadian painters who still had no choice but to subsidize their real work by teaching or by commercial art. Jock Macdonald dramatically belied the stereotype of the dour Scot. He was warm and unusually gregarious. His life had not been easy and his career as an artist-teacher had made him cynical about the politics of the art world. But this did not dampen his enthusiastic interest in life — nor did it ever affect his intense dedication to helping his students. This help often took the form of generous loans of money to young artists — loans which Macdonald could never really afford, but which were symbolic of his desire to encourage anyone who wanted to become an artist. William Ronald (pages 105-12), who studied under Macdonald, claims "there never was a better teacher." Ronald thinks that Jock's painting bloomed late in life, partly because he had expended a lifetime of energy on his students. Ronald says of Macdonald, "in a way teaching was his art."

As an artist, Macdonald—like Borduas—was isolated in his early training and work from the great mainstream of twentieth-century art. Like Borduas, Macdonald became fascinated by the spontaneous and unself-conscious communication of children's art and — again like Borduas — groped toward the same spontaneity by experiments in water colour: their tricky fluidity and the need for rapid execution made easier the sort of "controlled accident" he was seeking.

But the comparison with Borduas cannot be strained too far. There is no parallel to Borduas' sudden rebellion against the past and his own roots. It has been widely assumed that Macdonald underwent a conversion to abstract painting rather late in life as a result of studying with Hans Hofmann in New York. Hofmann, who had escaped the Nazis in the thirties to live and teach in New York and Provincetown, Mass., was a fervent exponent of abstract art. He talked passionately about the "forces" in painting. Painting had to do with "the heart and mind"; it must be full of "push and pull." These were ideas akin to Macdonald's own, and Macdonald did study briefly with Hofmann in the summers of '48 and '49. But in retrospect it is obvious that the Hofmann experience was merely another step in a long, steady evolution toward his final mature work.

Born in Thurso, Scotland, Macdonald served an apprenticeship as an architectural draughtsman, then took a design diploma at the Edinburgh College of Art and became staff designer for a firm of Scottish textile manufacturers. This training in purely formal design, rather than in the traditional drawing from casts and life, played a part in his later progress toward non-figurative art.

In 1925 he turned to teaching, and in 1926 he arrived in Canada to take over the Department of Design at the School of Decorative and Applied Arts in Vancouver. He found the atmosphere of the school stultifying and repressive and, except for his fellow-teacher Frederick Varley, he found the artistic community small and insular. He and Varley founded their own school, the British Columbia College of Arts. (Not very surprisingly, given their aggregate administrative talents, the school lasted only a year or so.) The second predicament was eased by the development of an informal group meeting at the home of a gallery owner for the purpose of music appreciation and philosophical discussion. The group turned out to have a strong interest in the philosophies of the Far East, as well as in other mystical and transcendental concepts such as Theosophy. Macdonald too became interested, especially in later years in E.S.P. All this while he had been going on sketching trips to various parts of British Columbia with Varley, and he had also met and formed close friendships with Emily Carr and Lawren Harris. Indeed, it was Harris who introduced Macdonald to Wassily Kandinsky's book, *Concerning the Spiritual in Art*, and the two spent many hours discussing transcendental philosophy and art.

Macdonald was still painting landscapes in the academic tradition, but with a strong design sense. Now, in this intellectual climate, he made his first essay into non-figurative art. Later he described the event (with his characteristic insouciant spelling) in a letter to a friend in 1956: "At that time, I was interested in colour and had been, for some time, carefully observing colour in flowers and plants. But I drew nothing on the canvas. I just started off with pure vermillion. Well do I remember doing it. I painted the canvas from the beginning to end without stopping to eat or rest. I was in an extasy and was pale and exhausted, but terribly exhilerated when I finished." He would never again be satisfied with painting mere outer forms.

The failure of the B.C. College of Arts forced Macdonald to go job-hunting again and, after filling various posts in Vancouver and Calgary, he finally moved his family to Toronto in 1947 and took up an appointment teaching and drawing at the Ontario College of Art. There he remained until his death.

In spite of his heavy teaching commitment, he continued the search for a means of expressing his own private transcendent reality. It was during the forties that he began his water colour experiments. At the same time he studied various European artistic developments, especially surrealism, and this led to a series of small paintings in water colours, inks and aniline dyes, which he called *automatics*. By the end of the forties he had transferred his explorations to the medium of oil and moved to a larger format.

By 1954 Macdonald was finding the academic atmosphere of O.C.A. so stifling that he thought once again of trying to set up his own art school. But in that year he received a Canadian Government Fellowship, which enabled him to go abroad for a much-needed break. After visiting England, the Macdonalds settled in Vence in the south of France, where he met Chagall and Dubuffet.

The latter encouraged Macdonald to continue his experimental water colours.

The stimulus of the overseas adventure led to an intense period of research into different media and during the first year back in Toronto he tried various acrylics and Duco. Finally Harold Town (pages 73-80) introduced him to Lucite and, because of its fluidity and flexibility, he continued to use it almost exclusively.

William Ronald, his former pupil, introduced him into the informal membership of Painters Eleven 1953-1959. Through this association, exhibiting opportunities were opened to Macdonald that would otherwise have been impossible for an abstract artist in the Toronto art community of those days. In addition, Ronald then went to New York and was established there by 1956, thus giving Macdonald his first real contact with the new centre of the international art world. There he met Clement Greenberg, a vehement apologist for colour-field painting. Macdonald invited him back to Toronto to meet the remaining members of the Painters Eleven group. Greenberg came, and the visit was important for Macdonald. He later wrote, "Greenberg gave me such a boost in confidence that I cannot remember ever knowing such a sudden development taking place before." His painting gained in the boldness and freedom and presence so evident in late works like *Heroic Mould* and *Fleeting Breath* (ill. p. 23) and he was painting at the height of his powers when he died of a heart attack in 1960, aged sixty-three.

Before he died, his work had entered several important collections, both private and institutional, and he had enjoyed a number of major exhibitions, including a retrospective at the Art Gallery of Ontario which, until that time, had never honoured any living artist except Group of Seven members with a one-man show. After his death the National Gallery also held a retrospective exhibition and, in her excellent essay in the show's catalogue, R. Ann Pollock wrote, "The last three years of Macdonald's life were, in many ways, his happiest and most productive. He was aware that he was finally achieving a personal style that would express all his feelings and ideas concerning life and nature."

Two other things are worth noting. Many Canadian artists and most teachers of art seem strangely reluctant to expose themselves firsthand to major international painting. They rarely turn up at galleries or museums to study the work hung there: it's as if they're afraid to face the implied challenge of the best. But Jock Macdonald was never afraid. He spent hours at the Art Gallery of Ontario and came to every gallery show. It seems an important thing to know about him.

But there is something equally important. It is a statement he once made for the catalogue of an exhibition. He wrote, "I must be true to myself or else I cease to be a creative artist." Then he added, "Apart from my own efforts in the field of art my greatest happiness is in the odd favourable opportunities I have to fight for the worthiness I sense in the work of younger artists. . . ."

Jock Macdonald
Russian Fantasy
water colour & ink on paper
9⅞'' x 13⅞''   1946
Art Gallery of Ontario
(Purchase, Peter Larkin Foundation, 1962),
Toronto

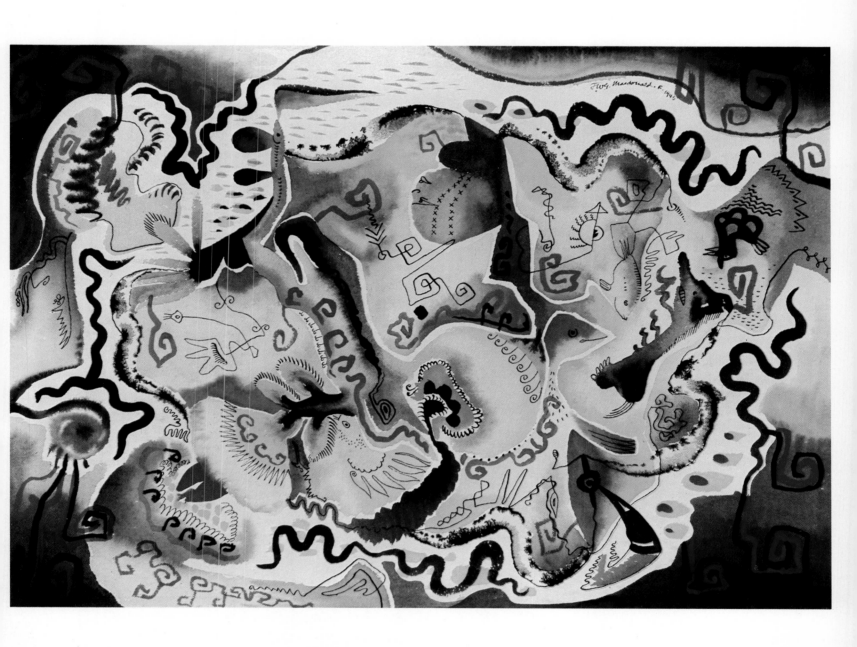

Jock Macdonald
Airy Journey
oil on canvas
42'' x 48''   1957
Hart House Permanent Collection,
Toronto

Jock Macdonald
Fleeting Breath
oil on canvas
48$\frac{1}{8}$'' x 58$\frac{3}{4}$''   1959
Art Gallery of Ontario
(Canada Council Joint Purchase Award, 1959),
Toronto

Jock Macdonald
All Things Prevail
oil on canvas
42″ x 48″   1960
National Gallery of Canada,
Ottawa

Paul-Emile Borduas

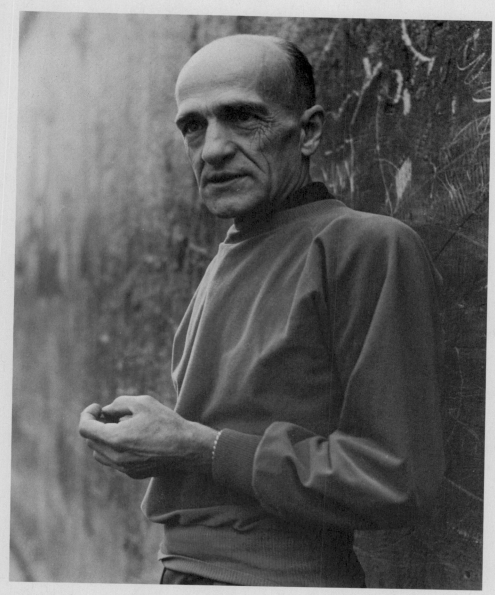

Refus de se taire — faites de nous ce qu'il vous plaira mais vous devez nous entendre — refus de la gloire, des honneurs (le premier consenti): stigmates de la nuisance, de l'inconscience, de la servilité. Refus de servir, d'être utilisables pour de telles fins. Refus de toute INTENTION, arme néfaste de la RAISON. A bas toutes deux, au second rang!

PLACE À LA MAGIE! PLACE AUX MYSTÈRES OBJECTIFS!
PLACE À L'AMOUR!
PLACE AUX NÉCESSITÉS!

Borduas has been likened to Jackson Pollock in the United States: the man who, by force of personality, intellectual rigour and sheer commitment, dragged Canadian painting into the twentieth century.

He was, in fact, far from the only Canadian trail-blazer. But for certain reasons he became a cultural hero to Canadian painters, particularly those of Quebec: an artist with symbolic, even mythic, significance. A bony, intense little man with a large head, an intent gaze from deep-set eyes, and a magnetic presence, he even looked the part. (As a teacher, he affected red turtle-neck sweaters in the classroom, when such gestures were defiant rather than modish.) He was the Artist in Revolt — and, in the eyes of most, martyred for his courage.

He was a dedicated, effective teacher (Jean-Paul Riopelle was a pupil), one of those passionate, enkindling theorists that the French call *animateurs*.

The eldest son in a family of a carpenter and metal-worker, Borduas began life in the little village of St. Hilaire, some twenty miles outside Montreal on the Richelieu River. He was bed-ridden with rheumatic fever when he was seven and he probably began drawing at this time, copying illustrations. After five years of schooling — the maximum available in the village — Borduas began working with his fellow-villager, Ozias Leduc. Leduc's work was very nearly of European stature, but it was circumscribed by the tradition of religious art so that Borduas' training was, in its way, as narrow and formal as any offered by the Canadian art academies of the day.

While continuing to work with Leduc, he earned his degree at L'Ecole des Beaux-Arts in Montreal and began to teach drawing. But, in 1928, he quit his teaching post and went to Paris. Though he left his Paris art school in disgust, and had trouble supporting himself through church-decoration commissions, he did discover the work of Braque, Soutine and Renoir.

Back in Montreal by 1932, he tried to live by his painting alone, but was unsuccessful; so he became a teacher of design in the primary schools. In the classroom he was greatly struck by the beautiful spontaneity of children's art. He struggled with his own art, trying for the same spontaneity, but he felt cramped by his upbringing, by the arid provincialism of Quebec and by the repressiveness of a clergy-dominated society. Of the whole decade of the thirties he later wrote, "In ten years of intense work only ten paintings were in any way worth keeping."

At one point, in an effort to escape his milieu, he wrote to the New Hebrides and Tahiti to ask about the possibilities of emigrating. The answers were discouraging so he stayed in Montreal, fighting it out, reading, thinking and speculating and trying to put his theories into practice. In 1937 he became a teacher of painting and art history at L'Ecole du Meuble, a design school with a reasonably progressive atmosphere. All this time, Borduas was still painting representational subjects. Then, in 1940, the invasion of France by Germany brought an influx of Parisians to Montreal. One was Père Couturier, a Dominican teacher and artist, who lectured for a year at L'Ecole du Meuble on all the latest ideas from Europe. Another was Borduas' contemporary and compatriot, Alfred Pellan (pages 33-40), who was returning after a decade in Paris and who proceeded to exhibit his avant-garde work.

In this atmosphere of ferment in 1941 — at the age of thirty-six — Borduas did his first abstract paintings. Later he wrote, "Children, always of great interest to me, opened up the way of surrealism, of automatic writing. The most perfect condition of the act of painting was finally unveiled."

Borduas' new non-figurative work began to attract important attention. This early work, with its organic and romantic spontaneity, is well illustrated by *Etat d'Ame* (ill. p. 29) and *Floraison Massive* (ill. p. 30). He started to sell his paintings during the forties and was especially encouraged when he made his first sale to a public institution, the Montreal Museum of Fine Arts. And he exhibited with increasing frequency in major shows outside his native province. Soon Borduas was enjoying an enthusiastic following of radical art students, young intellectuals and convinced collectors. It was from this coterie that the Montreal-based art movement known as Automatisme sprang. The label came from one of Borduas' own canvases, *Automatisme 1.47*, exhibited in a group show with his students in March 1947. Another Montreal painter, Guido Molinari (pages 161-8), has since insisted that *he* was the first to attempt truly automatic painting, having made experiments both blind-folded and with all the lights turned out in order to block off any communication between the hand and the compulsively judgemental eye. Be that as it may, Borduas' title was accepted at face value, and applied to the controversial title group: Les Automatistes. They included, besides Borduas, Barbeau, Fauteux, Garvreau, Leduc, Mousseaux and, eventually, Marcelle Ferron and Jean-Paul Riopelle. In the same year, 1947, an exhibition officially called *Automatisme* was organized by Riopelle and Leduc for La Galerie du Luxembourg in Paris. In reviewing the show, the late Guy Viau, later assistant director of the National Gallery, Ottawa, defined Automatisme with some scorn, thus: ". . . an imprecise and limited term to qualify the use, common to all painters, of chance discoveries, of forms which appear on a canvas without premeditation." Nonetheless, Borduas and the new pioneer avant-garde Montreal art movement had already won a toehold in Canadian art history.

This toehold was to be converted into a pedestal with the publication, in 1948, of the manifesto, *Refus Global*. It was written in French, and received little distribution outside the author's own province, but in Quebec it caused a furor.

A quarter of a century later it is difficult to comprehend why. *Refus Global* was simply a collection of plays and essays on political and social issues, taking its title from the introduction by Borduas himself, in which he summarized the philosophical position of the small group of discontented French-Canadian intellectuals with whom he had been associating. In it, Borduas pleaded for a mature sense of social responsibility and a complete rejection of all the traditional patterns of thinking. He was particularly critical of the established Church and the influence of organized religion. Compared to the prose of today's young revolutionaries, it was mild, calling not for the destruction of existing institutions, but only for an attitudinal realignment. Still, in the repressive and authoritarian atmosphere of Duplessis' Quebec in the forties, it took rare courage.

Borduas was fired from L'Ecole du Meuble for it. And so he became a martyr.

The next three years were very difficult. In 1949 Borduas entered hospital for a serious operation for stomach ulcers, undoubtedly brought on by the controversy. Added to ill-health were domestic and severe financial difficulties, and the sadness of seeing Les Automatistes drift apart and go their independent ways. In 1951 he scarcely painted at all.

Then, his health still impaired by the ulcer operation, he turned to water colours as being less demanding physically. And here his artistic development parallels Jock Macdonald's, for both men discovered a new freedom of expression at about the same stage by turning to this medium. Fortunately, also, at about the same time, the unusually devoted patronage of two Montreal collectors, M. and Mme. Gérard Lortie, gave him some financial freedom. Lortie, in fact, became a sort of unofficial business agent for Borduas, managing to sell, in all, some 150 Borduas paintings in Canada, two-thirds of them in Quebec, and many of them to people making their very first purchase of a work of art.

Thus provided for, Borduas was at last able to escape his native province. He went first to New York, where he met such leading figures of the abstract expressionist school as Willem de Kooning, Adolph Gottlieb, Robert Motherwell, Jackson Pollock and Franz Kline. Pollock and Kline, with their achievements in gestural painting, were undoubted influences.

In 1955, still searching, he moved on to Paris. After five productive years he died there of a heart attack in 1960.

Borduas never achieved Pollock's degree of accidental, purely gestural painting. Even with the floating images of his very last works, one feels the presence of a keen and critical mind, testing and adjusting each shape until it is just right. But he *was* attaining, in his last years, a synthesis of all those dogged experimental strivings which had marked his work from the beginning. And he was, in the larger air of Paris, managing to infuse into his big oils some of the freedom and grandeur he had discovered in his water colours. All the same, he died feeling exiled. To his patroness, Mme. Lortie, he wrote, "At this point I would give Paris and all the blessings of the earth for a small corner were it in Canada."

Paul-Emile Borduas
Etat d'Ame
oil on canvas
22$^{1}/_{4}$'' x 29$^{3}/_{4}$''   1945
M. & Mme. Gérard Lortie Collection,
Montreal

Paul-Emile Borduas
Floraison Massive
oil on canvas
25³/₄'' x 31⁷/₈''   1951
Art Gallery of Ontario
(Gift from the Albert H. Robson
Memorial Subscription Fund, 1951),
Toronto

Paul-Emile Borduas
Fragment d'Armure
oil on canvas
51″ x 77″   1957
Stephen Hahn Gallery Collection,
New York

Paul-Emile Borduas
L'Etoile Noire
oil on canvas
63¾'' x 51¼''   1957
Montreal Museum of Fine Art,
Montreal

Alfred Pellan

It is important to take all the time necessary to do the picture well. I admit to being a slow painter, provided that a good picture comes from it.

A painter should be able to master his resources: if you are not in control of the techniques, the techniques will control you.

When I was teaching I sharpened the awareness of my students, I sowed uneasiness, I stimulated research: and the students learned to observe, to question themselves, to make their own discoveries. Lacking the complex of the prophet or the manitou, I did not want disciples behind me.

It seems a peculiarly Canadian phenomenon that some of the country's most influential art teachers have been equally successful as artists – thus giving the lie to the old cliché that "those who can't, teach."

Pellan, the senior living artist of the twenty-four chosen for this book, ranks with Borduas and Macdonald as a Canadian artist-teacher. As a painter, his virtuosity is formidable, his vision unique and his work unmistakable. As a teacher he was among those pioneers who introduced into the hidebound provincialism of Canadian art circles some of the liberating explorations of contemporary European painting. And he did this at a crucial time, that is to say just when the Canadian landscape tradition originally inspired by the Group of Seven was dying and a great desire to break with tradition was stirring in Quebec.

But, unlike the other two teachers, Pellan seems to have been appreciated in his own lifetime in his country of origin, most probably because he had achieved a solid and even glamorous international reputation early in his career. From this unassailable base he was able to launch his catalytic career at home.

His was a precocious talent. Born just after the turn of the century, in Quebec City, he entered L'Ecole des Beaux Arts at the early age of seventeen and the same year, 1923, had his first work purchased by the National Gallery. In the next five years he proceeded to carry off many medals for painting, design, sculpture, sketching, advertising and anatomy – inside the school. Upon graduation he was awarded the first Province of Quebec Bursary to study at L'Ecole Supérieur Nationale des Beaux Arts de Paris, and thus he went to Paris. Except for a brief, unsuccessful trip back to Montreal in 1936 to see if a teaching post were available, Pellan remained in Paris studying and painting until 1940. He was strongly under the influence of the artistic giants of the European school; including Bonnard, Van Gogh, Picasso and, above all, the surrealists Max Ernst and Paul Klee. And he counted among his familiars such seminal figures of the modern movement as Corbusier and the cubist Ferdinand Leger.

The German invasion of France brought Pellan back to his own country and there he established himself in a studio in Montreal. In October of that year his work was exhibited at the Montreal Museum of Fine Arts. In many ways the exhibition was a crucial event in the Canadian art world, not least for the impression it made upon his contemporary, Borduas.

His paintings were strongly dominated by the many influences he had absorbed in Europe: fauvism, cubism, surrealism, abstraction. Yet Pellan's personal stamp was clear. His art was full of Gallic spirit, with highly decorative surfaces marked by the brilliant gypsy colours so reminiscent of French-Canadian village life. Here was a native son who had retained his own identity while bursting free of Quebec's parochial confines to join the international avant-garde.

In 1943 Pellan was given a teaching post at L'Ecole des Beaux Arts in Montreal. In time it became clear that his approach and interests differed from those of Borduas and Les Automatistes. In fact Borduas was later to write scornfully, "Pellan completely rejected surrealism which for us had been the great discovery. Pellan only believed in cubism which, somewhat thanks to him, had already lost its mystery for us."

Be that as it may, Pellan gradually gathered a group of followers in whom he created an awareness of those modern movements in European art which were shaping the course of twentieth-century art history but which were surprisingly little known in Canada at the time. Yet he encouraged his students to find their own imagery and explore its sources to the limit. He himself has written, "When I was teaching I sharpened the awareness of my students, I sowed uneasiness, I stimulated research: and the students learned to observe, to question themselves, to make their own discoveries. Lacking the complex of the prophet or the manitou, I did not want disciples behind me."

In 1952 Pellan received a Canadian Government scholarship which enabled him to revisit Paris and, in 1955, perhaps as a result of this renewed contact with the French art world, he was given a singular honour: a one-man exhibition at Le Musée d'Art Moderne in Paris. The tribute confirmed Pellan's reputation at home as one of the major figures in the Quebec art scene, and Canadian honours shortly followed. For example, the National Gallery organized a large retrospective exhibition for him in 1960. In 1967 he was made a Companion of the Order of Canada, and in 1968 he was given a senior fellowship from the Canada Council. In addition he holds honorary doctorates from three major Canadian universities.

He has exhibited on a world-wide scale and indeed his list of medals, awards and exhibitions is more extensive than that of any other Canadian artist. And his artistic development has been consistent and clear. The 1943 example of his work, *Femme d'une Pomme* (ill. p. 37) fairly bristles with clues to his European influences.

By the sixties the same influences are present but they have been absorbed and incorporated into the peculiar decorative, surrealist vision that has always made Pellan's work unique, if no longer avant-garde. His eclecticism, that is to say, now serves his own ends. With the possible exception of John Meredith (pages 145-52), no other artist among the twenty-four in this book produces work so recognizably individual.

Today, at sixty-six, Pellan lives with his beautiful young wife in Auteuil, Laval, P.Q. Short of stature, with a strong peasant face and quick, decisive movements, he is obviously a man of great physical strength and vitality. His manner is shrewd and urbane, in spite of the lumberjack shirts he likes to affect. Still painting as vigorously and prolifically as ever, he is the grand old man of the modern movement in Canada.

And yet there is an anomaly: his crucial importance goes unquestioned; his influence on Canadian art is almost universally respected; the contemporary painters of Quebec are outspoken in their admiration for his accomplishments. But the work itself?

When the Group of Seven were honoured by the *Fifty-Year Golden Anniversary* exhibition, a number of young artists attended the opening at the Art Gallery of Ontario in Toronto wearing T-shirts stencilled with the Group of Seven logo from the exhibition catalogue. They spoke affectionately and admiringly all evening of the importance of the Group. But they didn't look at the pictures. I think it's somewhat like this with today's Quebec painters and Pellan.

Alfred Pellan
Femme d'une Pomme
oil on canvas
63³⁄₈'' x 51¹⁄₁₆''   1946
Art Gallery of Ontario
(Gift from Mr. & Mrs.
Charles S. Band, 1956),
Toronto

Alfred Pellan
Ensemencement
oil on plywood
12″ x 36″   1961
L. J. Wildridge Collection,
Toronto

Alfred Pellan
Fines Tiges
oil on plywood
$11^{7}/_{8}''$ x $22^{7}/_{8}''$ 1964
Mr. Joel Roher Collection,
Toronto

Alfred Pellan
Végétaux Marins
oil on plywood
48$\frac{1}{8}$" x 32$\frac{1}{8}$"   1964
Art Collection Society of Kingston, Ontario

Jack Shadbolt

I think as I grow more experienced in painting, that my mind, to paraphrase Paul Klee, is less on form than on forming. At least I distrust too rigid a preconception. I court the unexpected and am prepared to change as I move. And yet, to further refer to Klee, I do "keep unbroken contact with my original idea". It works something like this: my private brain-storming sessions go on longer than they used to. I tend to roll an experience over and over, carrying it always with me until it has been sounded out from all angles and moods for its basic structural nature from which each of these is but a variant. When this basic structure has been thus reduced in my mind it emerges as a visual form configuration which embodies the whole idea. It is a concrete visible equivalent, say, of formal confrontation or subtle intertwining, explosive fusion, lyric illumination, monolithic forthrightness, regular or irregular intervals, conflicting or sympathetic resolutions of form, dissolving or declared presentation, rhythmic or static progressions, linear or massive delineation—it has been processed through the whole gamut until it emerges as 'right' or 'true' to what motivated it. In short it has been 'computerized' into a form-idea expressing a thematic concept.

Now I am in business. Coolly I can set about work. I know, by this time, the format, the basic colour mood, the texture and the quality of definition required — pictographic, graphic, loose or firm handling, what character of contrasts or sympathy to exploit — all of which have indicated what medium to employ. I sense out and faintly define the general format which with me is usually formal and hierarchic. I mentally rehearse my relays of procedure (and it is here that long experience of a medium is rewarding). I tune up my psyche and from then on I use all my craft and wits while performing at high speed. It is knowing my theme and its multiple overtones of possible variation that have enabled me to invent unpremeditated solutions, to follow subtleties that emanate from the work procedure itself as the form linkages suggest meaning linkages, and as the work reaches its state of seizure I do everything I can deftly and unobstrusively to assist it to walk off the sheet whole and alive.

If I feel sure that it has worked I whisk the painting out of sight and immediately plunge into a new version while my memory of the process is acute, but with a deliberately altered set of variables such as colour. In this way I am often immersed for some prolonged period in a set of variations on a theme. I have thus maintained unbroken contact with my original idea. The theme by now has become the 'grand theme' which is the equivalent of the old 'master work' and this gives me an assurance of stability and of dealing with larger relevance. I am freed by a wider implication from the original experience.

This parlaying process has become very much a part of my life-style. With it I can improvise freely from a firm point of departure. I can embrace ideas without losing my identity.

In the catalogue introduction for the National Gallery retrospective exhibition of Jack Shadbolt's work in 1969, Anthony Emery, Director of the Vancouver Art Gallery, wrote, "Shadbolt's position as a regional artist seems to me to be clear beyond any doubt: after Emily Carr he stands pre-eminent among Canadian artists who have lived and painted between the Great Lakes and the Pacific Coast." Emery went on to add, "In the late 1950s and early 1960s no Canadian painting show could be regarded as truly representative of the best that this country had to offer unless it included at least one work by Jack Shadbolt." That is still true today.

To call someone a regional artist is really no more than to say he uses the common language (well or badly as the case may be) but with a detectable regional accent. Jack Shadbolt paints with the West Coast accent. A biologist's intimacy with nature, a fascination with traditional Oriental painting and an interest in eastern mysticism have been peculiar to the West Coast school. Jack Shadbolt shares these concerns. (In addition he is a confirmed Vancouverite, which means that he loves the place and can scarcely be dragged away from it.) But his particular strength is his doggedly consistent exploration of his own perceptions. His *Red Knight* of 1947 (ill. p. 45) has, subject matter aside, many of the same purely visual preoccupations of his 1971 *Owl House Triptych* (ill. p. 48). The forms he deals with today have always concerned him, though they may have appeared in many different guises. And, no matter how abstract, Shadbolt's work has always been based upon his mysteriously emotional and highly subjective view of nature. He has written, "I find the very absorption with nature helps me to feel one mood at a time; such as the dry gold of autumn leaves, the dark earth of winter waiting, the crisp white of frost, the green sunlit burgeoning of spring." He has also written, in *In Search of Form* (McClelland and Stewart, Toronto, 1968), "I find that objects which most involve my interests, because they go deep into my experience and therefore command my closest attention, yield the most meaningful conceptions. This suggests to me that the whole involvement of an artist with his objects is more than just factual, structural or external. It may also be historical and sociological; but it even goes further into his most intimate responses to them. Why he chooses the objects he does, and how this subtly conditions the qualities with which he endows their portrayal — with austerity, tenderness, massiveness, etc. — can involve the whole range of emotional experience. Over my own choices I have little control."

Jack Shadbolt was born, only three years after Alfred Pellan, in Shoeburyness, England. But at the age of three his parents brought him out to Victoria, B.C., and there he grew up and got his education.

He became a high-school teacher, but while still at Provincial Normal School he was introduced to a circle whose interests were poetry, the theatre and art. Around this time he also met and formed a friendship with Emily Carr. And on his own he began to dabble in painting.

In 1933 he took a trip to Chicago, Detroit, Toronto and New York and, as he records it, "Saw Mile of American Art at Radio City and knew for the first time I was a committed artist."

His formal art education consisted of night classes for the next three years under Frederick Varley at the Vancouver School of Art and a year at schools in London and Paris. In 1938 he returned to the Vancouver School of Art where he taught, with interruptions including service as an official war artist, until resigning in 1966 to devote full time to his painting. He was a spell-binding teacher, the major teacher of western Canada, probably ranking in importance only after Borduas, Macdonald and Pellan. A big, muscular man, radiating the physical vitality of an outdoorsman and the intellectual presence of a university president, he had — and has — a formidable gift for talk. He is capable of talking till dawn, positive cadenzas of talk, on subjects ranging from Oriental calligraphy to the philosophy of education, all while pacing the room and pausing only to rummage through his books and papers and canvases for apt illustrations. It is an exhausting experience but a stimulating one. His talent for metaphor could have made him a poet; instead he turned it to the difficult task of communicating to students what can scarcely be communicated: how to go about painting. Indeed, he can almost make non-painters understand the process, as in this passage from *Art and Artist*: "The literal battle becomes the plastic battle, physical movement becomes form thrust and counterthrust; triumph becomes blazing colour, sharp contrast, and explosive space pressure. Release becomes expanding space, lifting movement; frustration becomes strangled form; suspense becomes static tension; joyfulness becomes rhythmic arabesque; power becomes monumentality."

That is the vocabulary of his own abstract expressionist paintings. His perennial theme is form: in one of his books he says, "I am the kind of artist who is incurably eager for form. I don't find forms, they find *me* ready and willing to take them over. My job is resisting. . . ." Only Shadbolt's subject matter changes. When he lived in downtown Vancouver he painted street scenes. When he moved to a beautiful wooded lot in suburban Capitol Hill, he turned to nature-cycle subjects. (He noted, "Wild excitement. Digging foundations and septic tank — experiencing layers of soil at eye-level; minute examination of life in grasses; genesis of cross-sectional underearth — horizon — sky preoccupations.") In the same way his visits to France and Italy and Greece have produced cycles of Mediterranean paintings.

Today, at sixty-three, Shadbolt is at the height of his creative powers: he himself, when discussing the choice of illustrations for this book, was insistent that his latest work be very well represented. And yet, unlike Jack Bush (pages 49-56), he has not disowned his earlier work, and in a way he comes back to it again and again, tackling the same problems from different directions and with new insights brought by experience. He is sensitive and open to the very latest avant-garde developments, perhaps partly because he is married to one of Canada's best curators of contemporary art, Doris Shadbolt of the Vancouver Art Gallery; and for this reason young artists continue to seek his advice and inspiration. But Shadbolt has never changed fashion.

Jack Shadbolt
Red Knight
oil & lucite on paper
29⁷/₈″ x 21¹/₄″ 1947
Mr. Ronald McDonald

Jack Shadbolt
Winter Theme No. 7
oil on canvas
39″ x 52″   1961
National Gallery of Canada,
Ottawa

Jack Shadbolt
Man of Symbol
ink crayon & latex
60″ x 40″   1971
Simon Fraser University,
Burnaby, B.C.

Jack Shadbolt
Owl House Triptych
mixed media, ink, chalk, latex
60'' x 120''   1971
Mr. & Mrs. Paul Heller Collection

Jack Bush

I have a song to sing — the best way I know how. If only six people listen — that's enough. I'm lucky — the six who listened and liked it are pretty keen on quality, and nothing short of top quality at that.

I would like to see more Canadians exposed to American and European competition. This was my good fortune. Riopelle and Borduas were before me. Caro is an ENGLISH sculptor. Noland is an AMERICAN painter. Bush is a CANADIAN painter . . . we have a great rapport.

To those who have followed his whole career as an artist, Jack Bush is something of a hero. His career, in fact, has been at least two careers. For many years he worked as an advertising artist who, on his own time, painted thoroughly competent and attractive landscapes and portraits. He had a secure place in the Canadian academic art establishment and solid status — precious to a man who make his living in commercial art — as a fine artist. He gambled it all. When he was already in his fifties he risked the outrage of his peers, the contempt of the public, the loss of his reputation and, above all, the real possibility of failure, to attack directly and on his own terms some of the major aesthetic problems that concern the towering international figures in modern art today. As a result he is now the best non-figurative painter in Canada.

Born in Toronto, Bush studied art in Montreal, 1926-8, under Edmund Dyonnet and Adam Sherriff Scott, and then in Toronto, at the Ontario College of Art, under Frederick Challener, John Alfsen and Charles Comfort. (The latter was teaching both as o.c.a. and at the University of Toronto at that time.) He went to work as an illustrator and advertising artist and was eventually so successful that he became a principal in the Toronto firm of Wookey, Bush and Winter. At the same time, outside working hours, he was drawing a great deal, especially from the model, and was developing his style in oil and water colour. The time was the twenties, and the influence of the Group of Seven was inescapable. Both visually and conceptually, his landscapes in oil throughout the period, and indeed until after World War II, remained reminiscent of the Group's work, though he had greater facility and technical competence than any of them. He was considered a successful artist of his generation, and duly became a member of the Ontario Society of Artists, an associate of the Royal Canadian Academy, a member of the Canadian Group of Painters and president of the Canadian Society of Painters in Water Colour. As a professional advertising man he was of course a member of the Art Directors Club.

In his drawing he developed a free, forceful and highly personal line; in his water colours he experimented with compositions and structural relationships worked out tonally. Unlike the experience of Borduas and Jock Macdonald, his experiments did not lead him directly into abstraction. He was working at a time when, and in a place where, in his own words, "parochial fences were high."

Oddly enough, it was the mass-circulation media that breached the fences. Popular magazines such as *Life,* which Bush saw as a matter of course in his business, began to carry colour illustrations and articles on living artists who were part of the evolving international modern movement. Bush recalls being particularly impressed by the works based on cubism, such as those of Lyonel Feininger and John Marin. Other Canadian artists were being similarly exposed for the first time to the avant-garde style, but for some reason Bush peculiarly felt the knowledge of international modernism as a special pressure on him.

He began to experiment with various forms of abstraction and surrealism and, in 1952, he made a pilgrimage to New York to see some of the actual works he had been studying in reproduction in the magazines. It was the first of a series of trips. Though still essentially figurative, his work throughout the whole decade of the fifties was influenced by what he saw during these New York trips and, understandably, it was uncertain, tentative and self-conscious. He was unhappy about it and honest enough to admit it — and courageous enough to start looking for help.

In the same year that he made his first New York pilgrimage, Bush participated in the *First Canadian All Abstract Exhibition* in Oshawa, Ontario. (Other artists in this book who were also included in the show were Jock Macdonald (pages 17-24), William Ronald (pages 105-12), Jack Shadbolt (pages 41-8) and Harold Town (pages 73-80.) The show led indirectly to his involvement with Painters Eleven, the informal group of Toronto-based abstract artists who joined forces in order to wrest exhibition space from the galleries and serious attention from the public. The group had no formal leader. But most of them were a generation younger than Bush, and Bush's establishment status and his business acumen were invaluable in getting them an audience and in organizing the logistics. He acted as secretary-treasurer. Bush exhibited with Painters Eleven from 1954 to 1959, and he called the meeting that officially voted to disband Painters Eleven. An explosive and ill-assorted collection of temperaments and credos, it had meant only to establish the point that *all* sorts of art were worthy of exhibition. Later Bush wrote of the experience, in a letter dated May 19, 1970: "And that was the end of Painters Eleven. A great and exciting eight years: we accomplished what we set out to do, and then each went our separate ways, grateful to each other for the fun it was."

Bush himself had ceased needing group support. In 1957, five years before Clement Greenberg's historic summer at the Emma Lake workshop, Painters Eleven had invited the New York art critic and colour-field enthusiast to Toronto to discuss their work. It was Greenberg who advised Bush to pursue the free and spontaneous direction indicated in his water colours. From this time onward Bush worked in thinly applied oil or acrylic and completely eschewed any recognizable forms. Greenberg's visit was a sort of road-to-Damascus experience for Bush. It was at this time that he faced up to the question every artist should ask himself: "Am I good enough?" Bush was truly prepared to quit if he found he was not worth consideration in open world competition rather than merely being admired as "a good regional painter."

In fact, to demonstrate his resolve, he turned his back on his own past. He resigned all his artist society memberships in 1964. In his officially-approved list of exhibitions, he has edited out all the shows in which he participated before 1954, except those with the Painters Eleven group. When asked by the Art Gallery of Ontario in early 1971 if he would permit the gallery to organize a full-dress retrospective, he was adamant that the exhibition should deal only with the years after 1950. (In fact he would have preferred the show to begin with 1960, as had a 1970 retrospective in western Canada.) The retrospective never did materialize because his doctor forbade it on the grounds that the nervous tension of his involvement would be dangerous for his health.

Consistent with his wishes, the work illustrated is all late. It gives no idea of the tentative and often uncertain results of his struggles towards self-discovery — let alone of his earliest "social realism." What it demonstrates is the way he has come to grips with some of the general compositional and stylistic concerns of contemporary international art, while still retaining and exploring his own authentic idiom: his subtle and carefully controlled tonalities, his conviction in drawing and his unique personal experience. He has suffered from serious angina since the late sixties, and he has said that certain bullet-shaped forms in his paintings about that time were hieroglyphs for the chest pains.

He has already been compared, both in his boldness and in his self-composure, to Matisse. (Bush once told Ken Noland that a work by Matisse was the most impressive thing he saw on a trip to Europe.) In a recent article in the *New York Times* (reprinted in the *Globe and Mail* for Thursday, March 2, 1972), Hilton Crammer, reviewing an exhibition of Bush's work in Boston, writes, "Bush has carried the development of colour-field painting into a very personal realm of expression that is in some ways closer to Matisse himself than to some of the Americans who have obviously acted as an influence. We shall, I have no doubt, be hearing a good deal more about Mr. Bush in the future, for he has taken a style that was often in danger of degenerating into an impersonal technical exercise and realigned it with the specifications of the experience."

Today, at sixty-two, Bush looks like a prosperous corporate executive but he paints with the exploring vigour of a youth. He is currently very worried about his wife's health, and lives a quiet, socially withdrawn life but — as he has since he made his total commitment to "big-attack" art — he is a fulltime painter who keeps a strict studio routine and exhibits constantly, both at home and abroad.

Despite his own uncertain health, he has the vitality of all those who are engaged upon big adventures. And he says, "My art . . . well, I've been lucky. A slow learner, I think the milieu of my middle period was exciting but somewhat of a waste of time, plus working commercially for a living. Two big breaks . . . a therapeutic session of many years freed me from oppression of local rules. Then I saw the outside world and contact with dedicated artists in other countries gave me the courage and encouragement to go on in my own way . . . for broke."

Jack Bush
Pink Blossom
oil on canvas
72'' x 70''   1965
Private Collection,
Toronto

Jack Bush
Dazzle Red
oil on canvas
81'' x 104''   1965
Art Gallery of Ontario
(Purchase, Corporations'
Subscription Endowment, 1966),
Toronto

Jack Bush
April Blue Green
acrylic on canvas
65″ x 86¹/₂″   1970
David Mirvish Gallery,
Toronto

Jack Bush
Strawberry
acrylic on canvas
68'' x 91''   1970
Mr. & Mrs. Alan Kotliar Collection,
Toronto

Alex Colville

I attempt to make my statement by my work.

Perhaps a succinct summation of Alex Colville is that his paintings are among the most written-about of any Canadian artist while Colville, himself, remains almost unknown, even in the small Maritime town in which he chooses to live.

Colville's paintings present a study in paradox: most are casein tempera and oil on Masonite, meticulously faithful in detail, with a clear, cool surface feel to them. Their subject matter, like the medium in which they are done, is open and light: a tree, a dog, a couple at the beach, a woman looking through binoculars. But under this reassuring surface is a tension, a sense that is almost sinister and that makes Colville's work deeply compelling.

Robert Fulford, in an issue of *Canadian Art* (January/February 1961) refers to the way Colville "holds his subjects in a revealing trance and, indeed, it is this trance which most distinguishes his art."

In reviewing Colville's first London show at the Old Bond Street Gallery of Marlborough Fine Art, critic Ursula Robertshaw says, in the January 1970 *London Illustrated News*, that his pictures "have an extraordinary atmosphere about them. Intensely still and lonely, they can invest even such a seemingly prosaic scene as a truck at a filling station with totemic significance. The huge lorry is too big for the picture; you see less than half of it. The pump attendant appears between the cabin of the truck and the container, a dwarfed figure with bandaged arm, anxious attention fixed on the observer. An Alsatian watchdog sniffs at the truck wheels in the foreground. A moment in time has been frozen against the molten gold of the evening sky, whose brilliant light pales the lit electric lamp and underlines the sombre colours of the truck, the man, and the dog. The vermilion of the pump at dead centre is like a deliberately crude comment, and the whole picture seems to be holding its breath."

Perhaps the latter is a little off the mark: it's not so much the paintings as it is the viewer, confronting even an inanimate object like a tree in a work by Colville, who holds his breath.

Colville's art cannot be tucked away nealy into a pigeonhole: it is not magic realism, renouncing as it does the obvious, the banal, the easy rural sentimentality of some romantic (and non-existent) past. Colville's magic is of a different kind. He depicts the "now" and remakes the visual world entirely, giving it a mysterious intensity that forces the view to ask questions about the nature of reality and about himself.

With Colville everything is larger than life, imbued with significance and magic which we ordinarily experience only occasionally and then usually as the aftermath of some traumatic event that has stripped up of the protective clichés with which we usually view the world. The most powerful aspect of Colville's work is its repeated ability to do this.

There is little in either Colville's background or education to provide clues to his penetrating inner vision: he was born in Toronto in 1920, eldest son of David Harrower Colville, an engineer who emigrated to Canada from Markininch, Scotland, and Florence Gault of Trenton, Ontario. The family moved to St. Catharines, where they lived until the artist was nine; the elder Colville's work then took him to Amherst, Nova Scotia. Alex Colville took his first art lessons there from a local teacher; from 1938 to 1942 he studied at the School of Fine and Applied Arts at Mount Allison University, in Sackville, New Brunswick, ten miles from Amherst. His studies were under the direction of an English painter, Stanley Royle; in 1942 Colville obtained his B.A. from Mount Allison but he feels now, and felt even then, that the art instruction he had received was not helpful, and he developed and studied on his own. He served in the Canadian Army from 1942 to 1944 and was subsequently attached to the Canadian Navy as a war artist, covering the landings in the south of France. Following this action he was promoted to the rank of captain and undertook a series of drawings, paintings and water colours done in Belgium, Holland and Germany. These are among the 126 of his works retained for the war collection of the National Gallery of Canada in Ottawa. In 1946, after his discharge, he was appointed assistant professor of painting at his alma mater.

Colville's first one-man show was at the New Brunswick Museum in Saint John, in 1951. By the mid-fifties, his work was being exhibited and reproduced extensively: at L'Exposition Internationale et Universelle de Bruxelles, Canadian Pavilion in 1958; at the 1961 Sixth Bienial de Sao Paulo. In 1963 he won one of the six prizes at the Dunn International Exhibition at the Beaverbrook Gallery in Fredericton. In that same year he retired from teaching to devote his full time to painting. In 1969, his work was exhibited at the Kestner Gesellschaft Gallery in Hanover; this introduction to the sophisticated art markets of western Europe, where Colville's work is eagerly bought, is one factor that has enabled him to support himself and his family entirely from the proceeds of his art.

In 1966, Colville was chosen to represent Canada at the Biennale di Venezia; he spent from September 1967 to June 1968 as Artist-in-Residence at the University of California's Santa Cruz campus. In 1971, he and his wife, the former Rhoda Wright of Kentville, N.S., travelled across Germany. *January* (ill. p. 64) is one of the works he painted on that journey.

The Colvilles, parents of three sons and a daughter, live quietly in a gracious old home in Sackville; Colville's works hang on the walls, though the place of honour, over the mantel, is given to a five-dollar reproduction of a Vermeer that the Colvilles picked up in the Hague at the time of the 1966 Venice Biennale.

It is worth noting that throughout Colville's working life, while art trends have come and gone internationally, he has pursued his realist vision without any apparent stress and strain.

In the 1967 collection, *Statements,** Colville astutely rejected the usual put-down of realist art: that it can be done more easily by photography. "It is important to realize", he wrote, "that a photograph is *taken* (ordinary speech reveals this — we say 'take' a photograph) whereas a painting is *made*. To *take* something is a form of abduction, kidnapping, or rape, whereas to *make* something as an artist is (I hope this is not too far-fetched) a kind of love-making — that is, it is only worthwhile to *make* that which one loves, respects, reveres or is captivated by. Also . . . what one is trying to make may not have existed in any objective way in ordinary life, but may be essentially a product of 'dreams, memories, recollections', to borrow Jung's terms — a kind of synthesizing of total experience. This cannot be 'taken' but has to be 'made'." [The italics are Colville's.]

The sense of "dreams, memories, recollections" is perhaps most stunningly evident in *Horse and Train* (ill. p. 62). This work, though more dreamlike in juxtaposition of subject matter, is far from surrealist; in the same way that Colville rejects the easy emotionality of magic realism, he refuses to deal in the now hackneyed pseudo-Freudian symbolism of surrealism, choosing instead the more difficult task of investing the immediate environment with forceful and personal meaning.

Foreign critics have suggested that Colville's evocation of certain aspects of the Canadian environment is so powerfully specific that he can be seen only as a Canadian artist. Robert Melville, the English art critic, very rightly rejects this view and says that Colville is "America's most distinguished realist painter since Edward Hopper." He goes on: "If some affinity between Colville and Hopper can be established, Colville must be seen to be the inheritor of an American realist tradition going back to George Caleb Bingham."

Statements: 18 Canadian Artists 1967. Norman Mackenzie Art Gallery, November 16-December 17, 1967.

Alex Colville
Horse and Train
glazed oil on panel
15³/₄″ x 21″   1954
Art Gallery of Hamilton
(Gift from the Dominion Foundries
& Steel Company Limited),
Hamilton

Alex Colville
Elm Tree at Horton Landing
oil on masonite
47⅞" x 35⅞"   1965
Art Gallery of Ontario
(Gift from the McLean Foundation, 1958),
Toronto

Alex Colville
Truck Stop
acrylic polymer emulsion on masonite
36'' x 36''   1966
Peter Ludwig & Wallraf-Richartz Museum,
Cologne

Alex Colville
January
acrylic polymer emulsion on masonite
24″ x 32″   1971
Collection of the artist

Jean-Paul Riopelle

Riopelle parle:

Je ne vois aucune différence entre le passé et le présent. Les oeuvres du passé ne sont ni plus loin ni plus près. Il n'y a pas eu d'évolution: ce qui s'est passé devrait simplement nous permettre de les voir mieux.

J'avais fait mon apprentissage, dessine comme un fou d'après nature. Mais can allait de moins en moins bien. Le dernier tableau que j'ai fait comme ça, je l'ait travaille pendant deux ans, sans pouvoir le finir. Je ne comprenais pas ce qui m'arrivait. Je ne savais pas que le type qui, aujourd'hui, veut dessiner un poisson sur une table n'y arrivera plus.

— Mais pourquoi?

— Parce qu'il y a perte d'intérêt. Je ne demande pas mieux que d'y croire, a son poisson — quoi de plus formidable qu'une truite de Courbet? — mais il ne peut pas m'y faire croire. Il fut un temps ou le rapport entre peintre et l'image était vivant, puis il l'a été moins; il ne l'était plus pour moi, en 1946.

— Progresses, c'est détruire ce qu'on croyait acquis (Recueilli par Pierre Schneider Catalogue de L'Exposition du Musée du Québec 1967).

Until the recent acclaim of Jack Bush through New York, Riopelle was undoubtedly Canada's best-known living artist both at home and abroad, a position justly earned by his creation of some of the most stunningly beautiful pyrotechnics in paint in Canadian art history. And he is still probably Canada's most successful artist in terms both of international recognition and of financial rewards. He lives in Paris, where he has made his home since 1948.

Riopelle was born in Montreal and grew up there. He began to paint at the age of thirteen and received regular lessons from a qualified art teacher all through his adolescence. The tutoring was utterly typical for the time and place. In Toronto, in the late twenties and early thirties, Arthur Lismer was already conducting experimental art classes for children, under the influence of the Swiss educational philosopher, Johann Heinrich Pestalozzi (1746-1827). Lismer disallowed copying of any kind and advocated free expression. But he was the exception. Riopelle's drawing-master was the rule: he set his pupil to copying *prints* of the old masters.

It was not until comparatively late in life that Riopelle was to see the originals of the works he was copying. And as for modern art, like all young Canadian art students, he was completely isolated from the twentieth-century mainstream. He did, however, become aware of the writings and work of the surrealist movement, as did Borduas, and this was the first serious influence of his career.

In 1943, he enrolled at L'Ecole des Beaux Arts in Montreal. But because of its academic and restrictive atmosphere, he and a group of his young student friends began to make a habit of visiting the much more progressive design school known as L'Ecole de Meuble. This is where Borduas had begun teaching in 1937 and was now beginning to assemble the disciples who would be known as Les Automatistes. The young Riopelle thus came very early under the master's influence. In 1946 he exhibited with the Automatise group — that is, with Borduas, Mousseau, Barbeau, Gauvreau and Leduc — marking his public break with official academic art. In the same year, with Leduc, he organized a showing of the group's work at La Galerie du Luxembourg in Paris. And in 1948 he was one of the co-signers of the manifesto *Refus Global* that was to prove so fateful for Borduas.

But Riopelle was already taking his own direction, in pursuit of the romantic and tragic dimension that contrasts so clearly with Borduas' questioning and philosophical impulse. In 1946 he had travelled outside the country to France and Germany. In the same year he paid a visit to New York, where he participated in an international surrealist exhibition. Jackson Pollock was coming into prominence at the time, but Riopelle denies the direct influence of Pollock, crediting rather — as does Guido Molinari (pages 161-8) — the research atmosphere of Montreal for his "arrival." Riopelle also repudiates the term "abstract" as applied to his non-figurative work, regarding the term as "une schématisation abusive."

In 1948, Riopelle settled in Paris and he has lived there ever since, already becoming in his own lifetime more than half a legend to his one-time compatriots.

His work fetch high prices. He is reported to live on a scale that includes several high-powered sport cars and a yacht. He is said to live the life of a bon-vivant, a familiar at bohemian-style parties that last all night. But he is said to alternate this with quiet fishing trips in remote areas. He is a shadowy expatriate figure. Though he periodically visits relatives in Montreal and often goes fishing and hunting in northern Quebec, he is practically unknown as a person or as an influence to the younger school of Canadian artists. This is in contrast to Michael Snow (pages 113-20), Les Levine or Joyce Wieland (pages 121-8), who may have left Canada but who return to exhibit here or to lecture and are consequently significant and esteemed leaders.

There are many who now consider that, in spite of his Canadian birth and rearing, Riopelle should be considered an artist of the School of Paris. In an exhibition of his work covering the period 1946-1970, held at Le Palais des Beaux Arts at Charleroi in 1971, all of the works displayed were borrowed from European collections, the majority being from private collections in Paris. No mention was made in the catalogue of his being a Canadian artist except by implication, in that the Canadian Cultural Attaché in Brussels was thanked for his expression of goodwill towards the exhibition.

On the other hand, Canada is anxious to claim him. Riopelle's work was included in the Canadian section of the Venice Biennale in 1954, and in 1962 the Canadian pavilion at Venice was given over entirely to his paintings and sculp-tures. It was on this occasion, and as a Canadian artist, that he was awarded the UNESCO prize. In 1963, the National Gallery of Canada gave him a comprehensive exhibition. And, in 1967, the year of Expo, no less official a Canadian figure than the Minister for Cultural Affairs, Jean-Noël Tremblay, claimed for Riopelle that, "The most celebrated Canadian painter is at the same time the most Canadian of our painters." Tremblay supported this view with the observation that, "As long as he lives, every great artist obeys his earliest influences and remains faith-ful to the deepest impressions that touched his childhood."

Knowing of his early interest in the paintings of Van Gogh, it is tempting to see in Riopelle's colouring, brushwork and heavy impasto the continuing influ-ence of the passionate Van Gogh. Some, though, have seen the influence of French mediaeval stained-glass windows in his work. Others insist on the influence of the rugged Canadian landscape, particularly the forests of his native province as he sees them on his fall hunting trips. The nationality of a landscape is problematic, but it *is* obviously nature, and not our modern technological environment, that moves him to produce these poetic painterly surfaces (ill. p. 70). As proof one has only to scan the titles of his work: *La Montagne, La Cavée, Avalanche, Hibou-Stoney Creek*. Riopelle has always worked in a wide variety of media, but he added to his traditional experiments in assemblage and collage, water colours and prints and an excursion into sculpture in the sixties, casting in bronze the same sort of free-form natural, almost accidental, agitated shapes that dominate his two-dimensional work.

Perhaps the truth is that Riopelle should be regarded as the truly international artist, paying small tribute to nationalism — either his own, that of New York or, for that matter, that of France, where his painting is more easily indentifiable through the New York school than the French.

Jean-Paul Riopelle
Sous Bois
oil on canvas
51³⁄₁₆'' x 78³⁄₄''   1948
Collection of the artist

Jean-Paul Riopelle
Pavane (triptych)
oil on canvas
centre panel: 118″ x 59″,
wings: 118″ x 79″
1954
National Gallery of Canada,
Ottawa

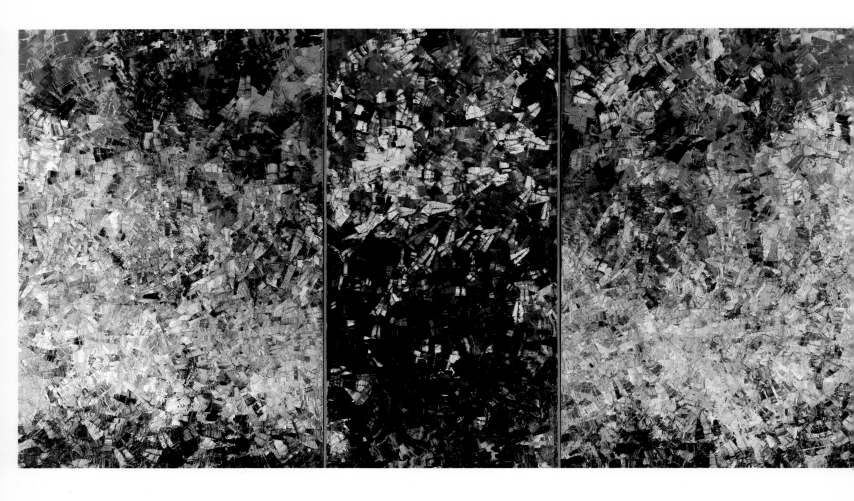

Jean-Paul Riopelle
Painting
oil on canvas
72″ x 108″   1956-7
Toronto-Dominion Bank,
Toronto

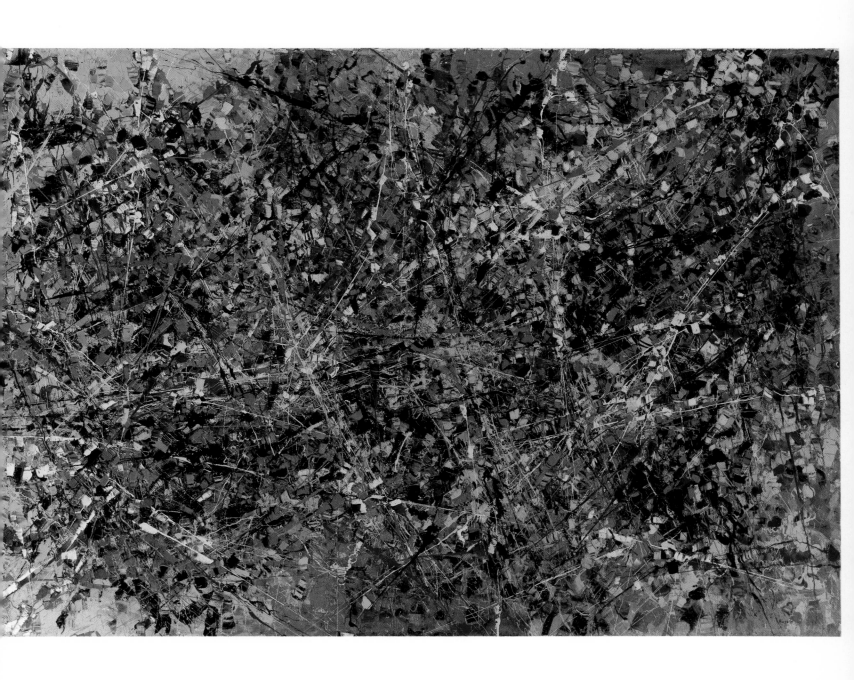

Jean-Paul Riopelle
Painting
oil on canvas
51¼″ x 76⅞″   1960
Art Gallery of Ontario,
Toronto

Harold Town

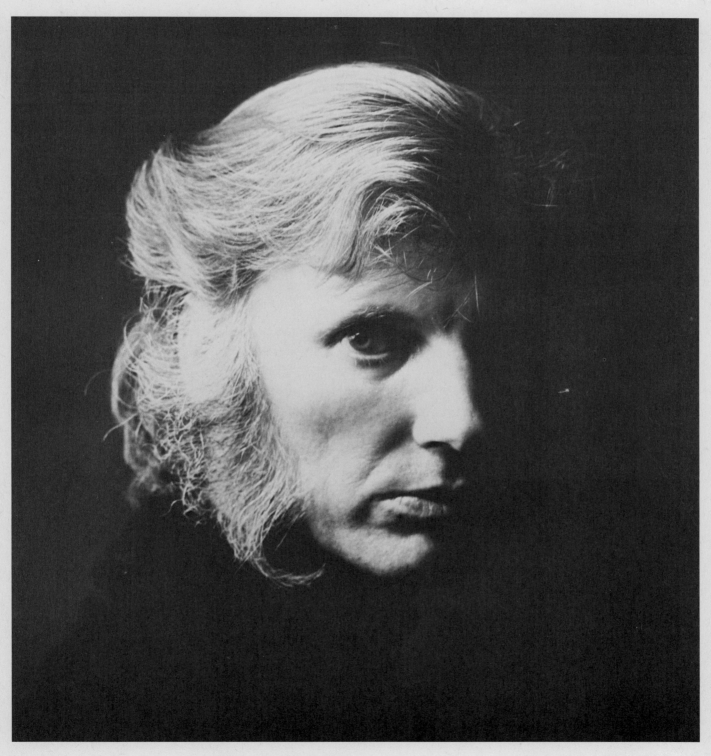

I paint to defy death.

There are two Harold Towns. Some would say there are more than that, but two is the figure to which Town himself admits.

One Harold Town is the public figure: a kind of *enfant terrible* of the Canadian art scene, flamboyant, and mischievous. In this *persona* he is always prepared to leap into an artistic skirmish, honed epigram to hand; he is un-afraid of controversy, or of making public gestures, including the cocked snook. His interests seem omnivorous, from health foods to old movies, and he is opinionated about every one of them. He is an outspoken performer, a dedicated pamphleteer and a published author who writes so colourfully that when he was given an Honorary Doctorate in Letters from York University recently, the public was unsure if he had received it for his writing or his art. It was for both. He also has a reputation, not entirely uncultivated, as a party-goer, a dandy and a rip. Consequently, he is much sought after by the media, and is lionized by the Toronto cultural establishment. In addition, he is an artist of such virtuosity, facility and output that he has been called "the Picasso of Canada." He has turned his hand to illustration, printmaking, collage and costume and scene design for the theatre, as well as drawing and painting. His exhibitions, medals, honours and awards are so many as to defy complete listing. He is clearly some-thing of a legend in his own time. (The legend includes the widespread belief that he never leaves Toronto. In fact he has travelled a good deal in the u.s. and knows both Chicago and New York very well; he stayed in New York for several months in 1948, when one could still walk the streets, and did so "night and day, eating up the sights." On the other hand, he does admit to fearing the "distraction" of travel.)

The other Harold Town is an intensely private man, reflective and profound, a good husband and father, a passionately loyal friend and a compulsive worker. His work habits are as regular as any factory worker's, with three long stints fitted into his day, which began at 11 a.m. and ends at 4 a.m. He spends many more hours alone in his studio than are ever spent in company.

Both Towns are present in his work.

The painting *Stretch,* 1971 (ill. p. 79), is one of a series of which the artist says, "Everything stretches in our society; this picture is about pulling cellophane out of a box, or spilling ketchup." It's also about Harold Town, with his intellectuality and his fantastic facility. Of the four illustrated, though, *Great Divide* (ill. p. 78) is perhaps the most typical Town: the aggressively eccentric composition; the theatrical contrast between the fine, nervous line (a reminder of the painter's superlative draftsmanship) and the arbitrary, harsh and geometric intrusions from the edges — all this against a background of handpainted little doughnuts obsessively repeated. Surely an expression of work addiction, the true ethic of wasp Toronto.

Town grew up the WASP kid in a tough district: a working-class area of midtown Toronto. He remembers drawing from earliest infancy and being encouraged in this – though rarely praised – by both his parents. They were unusual, for in the Depression years in Canada the profession of artist was low on the list of occupations preferred by parents for their children. His mother never seemed to have an idle moment; and she painted a bit, even if it meant doing the ironing at midnight. Town remembers his father as always "fierce" towards him, unwilling or unable to show his son the real pride he felt for Harold's accomplishments. But he was a diligent and fastidious worker at the various trades forced on him by the Depression; for example, he painted houses for a mere twenty dollars, but insisted on applying three or even four coats – and taught his son at the same time how to "sweep" the brush in fluent strokes. Town attributes his own drive to his father's example. Even today, he regards any day spent without working at his art as "a day of guilt."

A slight, blond, talky youngster, Town might have been bullied at the neighbourhood school except that he was "class artist," which gave him status. After public school, he attended Western Technical School, where he "majored" in art and, on graduation, entered the third year at the Ontario College of Art. He says it was a great time to be at the college because it was wartime by now and most of the teachers had left. It is obvious that his artistic development owes nothing specific to any teaching he received.

Town earned his living until he was at least thirty by doing store display, advertisements, magazine covers, etc. His father's son, it was unthinkable to him not to be self-supporting and so he made the compromise typically forced on the Canadian artist in the forties and early fifties: he subsidized his real vocation by working as a commercial artist. His "fine art" he pursued on his own time, with inadequate studio space and very little hope of getting his work exhibited. It was during this period that the Town legend began to develop. Struggling to keep alive as an artist, he accepted many invitations in order to enjoy free food and drink. In turn, he held his liquor well, and was consistently witty, vociferous and entertaining, which led to more invitations – and to his growing reputation as a party-goer.

Nonetheless, it was a lonely and frustrating period for a serious abstract artist. In spite of Town's fierce independence, he did accept membership in the R.C.A., the Ontario Society of Artists, the Canadian Group of Painters and the Art Directors Club. But he was active only in one group: the short-lived Painters Eleven. He was their writer and propagandist; in turn their creation of group opportunities to exhibit gave him his first real public exposure. His reputation as a painter began with Painters Eleven in 1952. In 1954, as the result of a chance meeting with Douglas Duncan, he was given a one-man show at the Picture Loan Society gallery. As early as 1956 he exhibited abroad at the Venice Biennale; in 1957 he was able to give up commercial art to become a full-time artist. Since that time his group and one-man exhibitions, both in Canada and internationally, have reached truly formidable numbers.

He is an undoubted "best-seller," living today with his wife and two daughters in a substantial midtown house, not many blocks from where he grew up but in a thoroughly upper-class WASP enclave. He has two studios in his home and two in the old Group of Seven studio on Severn Street, to which he walks, arriving compulsively each day on the stroke of 1 p.m. His evening and nighttime stints are separated by a spell of watching old movies on television: he is a movie buff with a vast store of memorabilia and lore to draw on, and he has written with knowledge and affection on the subject.

Town's ability as a draftsman is undisputed. And his single autographic prints, produced between 1955 and 1957, were surely among the most beautiful art objects ever made by a Canadian artist. But his paintings have been more controversial. His large canvases of the early sixties must rank as powerful and compelling images. But the critics since have been as varied in their attitudes towards his talent as the talent itself is varied.

Town himself has never been cowed by the critics, and has never been afraid to leave a successful "style" to pursue his own virtuosity. He has, indeed, often deliberately challenged himself to try the impossible.

No book on Canadian painting of the period 1945-70 would be complete without him.

Harold Town
The Fence
oil & lucite on linen
80¼'' x 108''   1959-60
Robert McLaughlin Gallery,
Oshawa

Harold Town
Great Divide
oil & lucite on canvas
90" x 60"   1965
Art Gallery of Ontario
(Purchase, Corporations'
Subscription Endowment, 1966),
Toronto

Harold Town
Stretch #27
oil & lucite on canvas
82'' x 74''   1971
Collection of the artist

Harold Town
Park #6
oil & lucite on canvas
70″ x 70″   1971
Collection of the artist

Ronald Bloore

I really, in a sense, don't think about it at all. It's not my problem to worry about it (work) ... it just goes on and on. When people say to me "You are down to twenty white lines on a white page"? "What's the next phase?" ... That is not their problem ... that is my problem.

Although sometimes I wonder about it when I get back to work again ... I work in cycles.

I do not worry about it ... solutions come first. I begin to find I have a vocabulary of basic elements and use a kind of visual language ... a visual alphabet. I don't care about the past.

Ronald Bloore is a thin, aloof man in his mid-forties, with the face of an ascetic or a priest. He made up his mind to be an artist at the age of four-and-a-half. For a while his work was perceptibly romantic and colourful (ill. p. 85 and p. 86), but for almost a decade now he has produced disciplined white-on-white "blind embosses" in related series. Some series are relatively poetic, and rich in associative material such as crystalline or snow-flake forms (ill. p. 87). But there are other series in which the motif is austerely restricted to parallel lines or, to be more precise, parallel ridges. Not long ago Bloore commented, "I begin to find I have a vocabulary of basic elements, and use a kind of visual language . . . a visual alphabet." He has also said, "When people say to me 'You are down to twenty white lines on a white board. What's the next phase?' that is not their problem. That is *my* problem."

Bloore deserves a place in any book on painting in Canada 1945-1972 if only for his single-minded pursuit of an artistic ideal. He is as uncompromising a man as he is an artist, and he and his work burn with cool integrity. But Bloore is also significant because of his role in the formation and development of the informal group that came to be known in the early sixties as the Regina Five. (Mindful also of the Group of Seven and Painters Eleven, Bloore is apt to claim facetiously that Canadians paint by numbers.) It was an extraordinary flowering of creativity in an unlikely art centre and Bloore's leadership, though disputed, was important.

Bloore was born of English parents at Brampton, Ontario. His decision to be an artist was precocious, but he remembers no artistic influence in his early childhood. He does remember that the boredom of high school in Brampton was alleviated for him by the study of certain Victorian paintings, unrelievedly bad, that decorated the corridors.

He left Brampton at seventeen and a half to join the RCAF, ended up driving trucks for the army instead, and finally was sent to telegraphy school. At war's end the best way to get a speedy discharge was to go back to school. Bloore enrolled in Art and Archaeology at the University of Toronto, a course that confirmed his broad interests in cultural history and in antiquity. These have been a persistent and sustaining influence on both his work and his thinking. He responded to his university years to such a degree that he has been drawn to Academe all his life. When Bloore graduated in 1949 with two scholarships, one to the University of Ottawa and one to New York University of Fine Arts, he chose the latter. At the time, what painting he did was not a primary concern.

For the next nine years his milieu remained academic, for he studied in the U.S. and Europe and lectured both at Washington University in St. Louis and at the University of Toronto.

Then, in 1958, he was appointed director of the Norman Mackenzie Art Gallery, attached to the Regina campus of the University of Saskatchewan. The post attracted him because the gallery went beyond art to museum functions as well. Bloore quickly established himself as one of the most controversial and far-out gallery directors of the day. He believed his role was to present to the community the whole spectrum of aesthetic experience, from sculpture to architecture, from ancient to modern, including the best and most advanced work being done in other parts of Canada. The important thing was to expose Regina to a range of outside influences to counter its isolation, and to set standards of quality.

It was as part of this program that he almost immediately became involved in organizing the summer sessions, held north of Prince Albert near Prince Albert National Park, known as the Emma Lake workshops. (See introduction.) He and his colleagues at the art school connected with the gallery invited the avant-garde American painter Barnett Newman to lead the seminar in the summer of 1959.

Newman brought none of his paintings with him to Saskatchewan and did no painting during the summer, but his personality and his ideas were catalytic. He gave the artists connected with the Regina School of Art a new view of themselves as artists, and was the central factor in the creation of the Regina Five. They included Bloore, Kenneth Lochhead (pages 97-104), Ted Godwin (pages 153-60) Arthur McKay and Douglas Morton. In addition Roy Kiyooka (pages 89-96) was involved with Bloore and McKay in issuing the invitation to Newman but subsequently left for Vancouver.

In succeeding summers other outstanding American artists were invited as guests and then, in 1962, acting on a suggestion from Barnett Newman, Bloore broke with tradition and invited a critic to run the seminar. The critic was the powerful and opinionated Clement Greenberg, godfather of colour-field painting and an advocate of the artist as the discoverer of solutions to purely formal problems.

1963 became a fateful year both for Bloore and for the Regina Five. He himself spent the year on the Greek island of Lesbos, on a Canada Council grant. Here his continuing archaeological interest attracted him to wall-painting, and to geometric relationships related to the golden mean. When he returned to Regina he destroyed all his former paintings and began working exclusively on Masonite, as giving a wall-like stability, and in "white on white" (although he had painted some white works as early as 1958), using an almost sculptural method to build up his surfaces. He had thus reached a turning point in his art.

He had reached a turning point in his career as well. He returned to find friends all converted by Greenberg to "instant" colour-field painting. Furthermore, Greenberg had recommended and helped arrange a program of exhibitions for the art gallery which was contrary to Bloore's ideals for the institution. Greenberg also wanted to sell Lipchitz' *Mother and Child* from the collection as "old-fashioned"!

At this embattled moment, Bloore was visited in Regina by Donella Taylor, a leading member of the Women's Committee of the Art Gallery of Toronto, and Dorothy Cameron, Toronto art dealer and animateur. "A pair of sharpies if I ever saw two," says Bloore, reflecting amusedly upon their somewhat spectacular entrance into his little gallery. Miss Cameron became Bloore's dealer and was instrumental in getting him to leave Regina for a post at York University in Toronto. He now lectures on "The Intellectual History of Mankind" and the "Visual History of Eastern Man" and paints on his own time.

After his summer in Saskatchewan Clement Greenberg rightly praised Bloore for having the same sort of integrity as Paul-Emile Borduas and, through the forces of this positive influence, keeping the Regina Five free from the superficial and faddish influences emanating from New York. At the same time he did not like Bloore's work, finding it "a little sour" and "too elegant in its impasted whites."

The elegance is undeniable. The sourness is open to question: rather, there seems a knife-edge balance between the Apollonian and the Dionysian in those arctic expanses, a disturbing shiver of tension between sensuousness and formal severity. In the end the viewer is left to read them hot or cool as his mood or temperament dictate.

Bloore is not prolific. His methods are perforce slow and painstaking, and he thinks out each painting in advance. Furthermore, he is, as might be guessed, a perfectionist whose attitude to his work is almost religious. If Borduas can be called a Jansenist then Bloore might be accused of being Calvinist. For himself, he says with the mixture of modesty and self-awareness one finds in many serious artists, "When I am old and rich, in the sense of being mature, I might begin to make images that are worthwhile."

Ronald Bloore
Painting
oil on masonite
48″ x 48″   1960
Jessie & Percy Waxer Collection,
Toronto

Ronald Bloore
Painting
oil on masonite
48'' x 48''   1961
Mr. & Mrs. Michael Taylor Collection,
Toronto

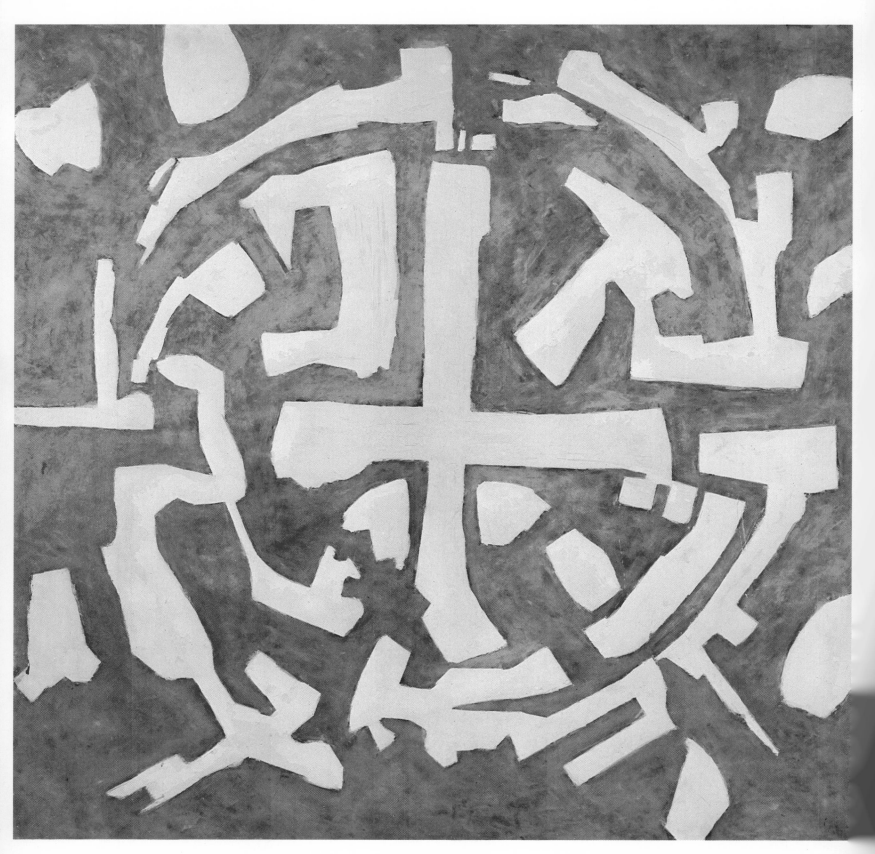

Ronald Bloore
White Mural
oil on masonite
142³/₄″ x 146¹/₂″   1967
Confederation Art Gallery & Museum,
Charlottetown, P.E.I.

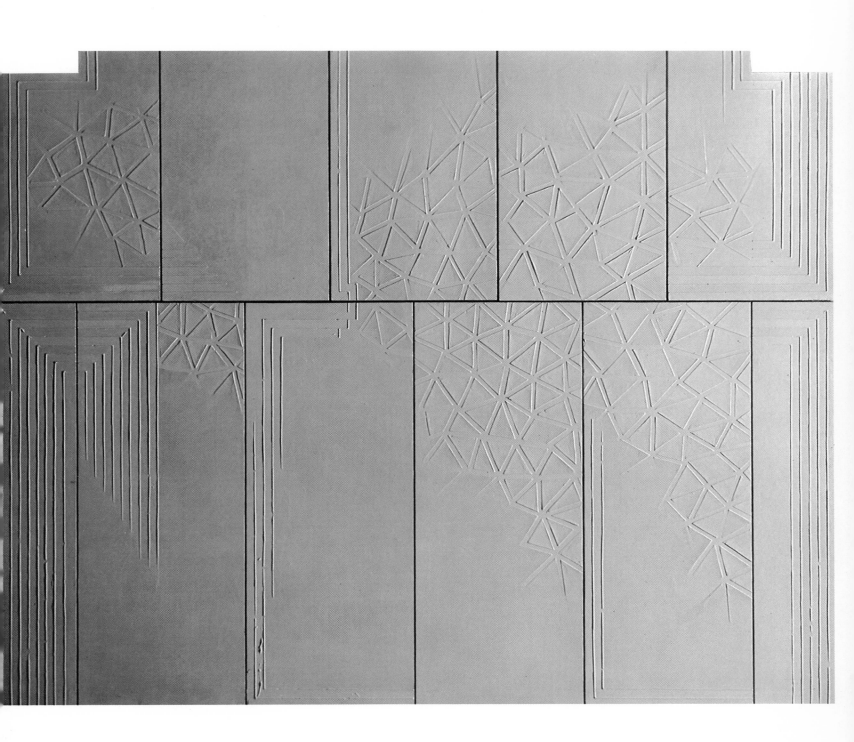

Ronald Bloore
Painting
oil & spray enamel on masonite
96″ x 43″   1971
Collection of the artist

Roy Kiyooka

In so far as I have not painted since the winter of 1969 — I do not think of myself as a painter but simply as an artist or artisan . . . a person who is interested in doing a number of different things. Hopefully they will fit together as a composite view portraying my singularity.

I now prefer that a stress be laid on the diverse thing that I am into . . . of course there will be overlaps.

I have always considered it an important part of what I am about in the fact of my having taught for nearly two decades.

During that time I have had the extraordinary pleasure of having taught some brilliant girls and boys who have subsequently gone on to do their own things in their own utterly inimitable fashion. There are the others who are more numerous with whom my life crisscrosses thru the breadth of this country.

This is taken in front of a very old house when all this started to happen. The house does not exist anymore and I doubt if the man taken in front of it does either —

Kiyooka claims he has always been an artist. At the age of eleven he copied the illustrations by C. W. Jeffreys that filled the history books being used in Canadian schools at the time. He remembers winning a prize for a detailed drawing of the milk-bottling machinery at a dairy in Calgary. And while still at school he drew a weekly comic strip for his classmates. The hero of this strip, based on the exploits of Superman who had become popular about that time, was called The Phantom.

The reference points of such childhood recollections seem thoroughly Canadian/North American. Ronald Bloore, who knew him in Regina, has remarked that Kiyooka sometimes seemed more prairie-minded and Canadian than a Saskatchewan native. Yet Kiyooka's parents were both Japanese. He himself speaks Japanese, visits Japan frequently and has an intense interest in Japanese culture, especially Oriental philosophy. And the dual sensibility thus suggested can be traced in Kiyooka's artistic development.

His earlier work, like *Barometer #2* (ill. p. 94), is still part of the mainstream of international hard-ege. And technically his paintings of the late sixties stand somewhere between those of the Montreal neo-plasticiens such as Guido Molinari (pages 161-8) and the work of the colour-field painters such as Ken Lochhead (pages 97-104). But what makes them different from both is a cool, contemplative mystery, a poise, that few of his peers can match. His characteristic ellipses are perfectly lyrical, precisely balanced by the rectangular grounds in which they float. *Plaeides* (ill. p. 96) is a good example. It is a feat of hand and eye that combines Oriental spatial sense with North American bravura. This is Kiyooka's special contribution as an artist. As a teacher — and he is something of a "guru" to regional Canadian painters — his contribution is an intellectual and spiritual commitment to internationalism in art.

Kiyooka was born into a large family of Japanese Canadians. His father had come from Japan at the turn of the century but, during World War II, the family was one of those moved by the government from the coast of B.C. to the prairies, where Kiyooka's father, who knew very little about agriculture, was forced to farm. The experience was traumatic for the whole family. A younger brother, Harry, was born in Calgary and is now also a distinguished artist, teacher and philosopher.

Kiyooka's first serious art education was at the Provincial Institute of Technology and Art in Calgary, where he studied from 1946 to 1949. This coincided with Jock Macdonald's short sojourn there and he was one of Kiyooka's teachers.

In 1955 he won a scholarship to the Institute Allende in Mexico, where he studied painting, drawing and fresco mural techniques with James Pinto. During the summers of 1955 to 1960 he attended the artists' workshops at Emma Lake, Saskatchewan, and there he worked successively under Joe Plaskett, Will Barnet, Herman Cherry and Barnett Newman.

Partly as a result of the Emma Lake experience, and partly through his own deepening interest in eastern philosophy and poetry, Kiyooka's paintings became more detached and cool. He moved to Vancouver in 1959 and soon became a leader in the awakening artistic community there. With his big, flat, colour-field paintings, he represented an internationalism both of style and ambition which made a powerful impact on the more regionally-oriented artists. He has since had the same impact on other Canadian centres for, unlike many Canadian teachers, he has moved back and forth across the country.

Kiyooka began as a gestural painter, but by 1961 his painting had started to assume the disciplined minimal quality for which it is known today. Since that time public recognition has gone hand-in-hand with his progress.

In 1961 he was included in the National Gallery's Annual Biennial. In 1962 he was included in an exhibition, called *Five Japanese Painters,* which was shown at Hart House, University of Toronto, as well as in Seattle, Vancouver and Montreal. By 1965 his work was regularly exhibited all over Canada and at the Grippi-Wardell Gallery in New York City. He was one of four Canadians to be shown at the Sao Paulo Biennial of 1966, and won an honourable mention with silver medal there. The same year his commercial gallery in New York gave him a one-man show. In 1967 his work was exhibited at Expo and in every major centennial show across the country. In 1968 he was included in several shows in Canada as well as the exhibition called *Canada 101* at the Edinburgh Festival.

In 1969 he won a commission to make sculpture for the International Exposition at Osaka, and ceased painting for the time being.

In fact he turned not only to sculpture (his sculptures, incidentally, are closely related to the aims of his last paintings) but to poetry as well. For many years he had been almost as interested in poetry as in painting and in recent years claims to have spent as much time in writing as on anything else. Two small books of his poems have been printed and at Sir George Williams University, Montreal, where he was Associate Professor in Fine Arts, Head of the Painting/Drawing section, he and four members of the English department organized bi-monthly poetry readings for four years. Kiyooka himself has given a number of readings.

In addition, Kiyooka has ventured into photography, which he makes into compositions with poems. He is thus thoroughly representative of that new generation of artists who are pushing beyond painting to explore the whole aesthetic experience. A note sent by Kiyooka while this book was in preparation is a revealing glimpse of his views (and of his delightfully unedited and unpretentious style): "let me know if its (the book) all abt only paintings or it is goin' to be also abt other things most of us (also) do thats not incidental to ART but part of it part of that huge whole art is."

Kiyooka is currently on a Canada Council senior grant coincident with a leave of absence from Sir George Williams. He says he is still painting, but the nature of this new work is unknown.

Roy Kiyooka
Aleph #2
aquatex on canvas
68$\frac{1}{4}$" x 93$\frac{3}{4}$"   1964
National Gallery of Canada,
Ottawa

Roy Kiyooka
Barometer #2
polymer (aquatex) on canvas
97″ x 69″   1964
Art Gallery of Ontario
(Gift from the McLean Foundation, 1964),
Toronto

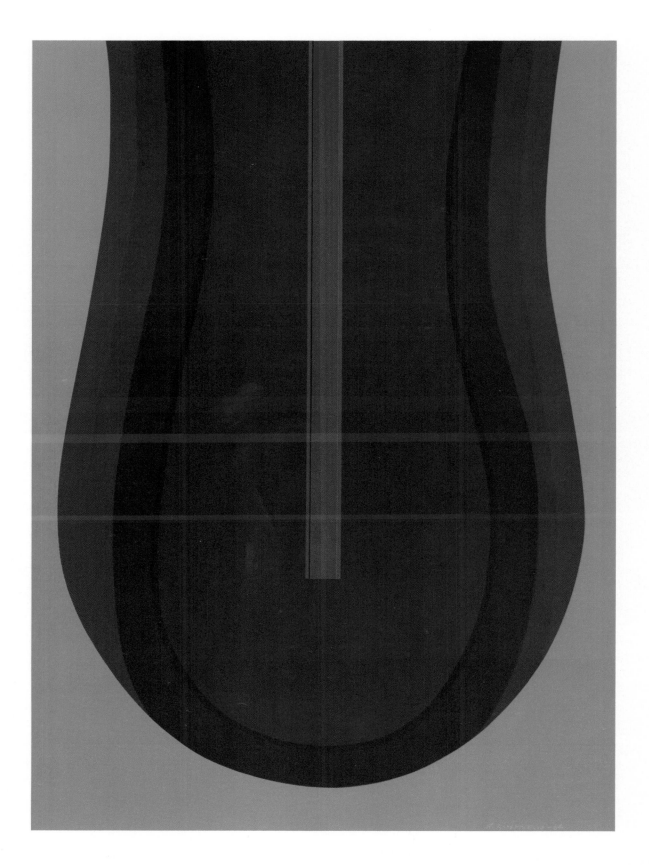

Roy Kiyooka
Homage to Debussy
acrylic on canvas
40″ x 120″   1966
York University,
Toronto

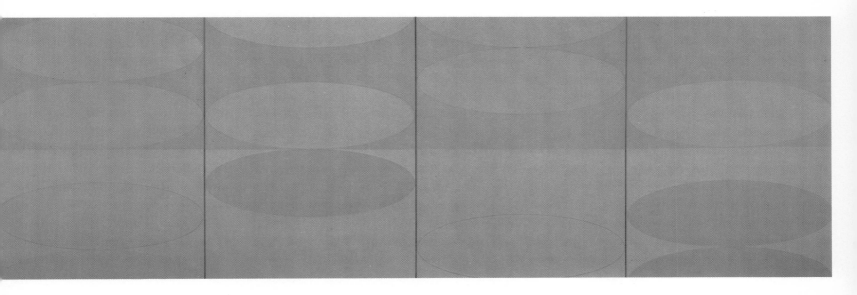

Roy Kiyooka
Plaeides
acrylic on canvas
72″ x 180″   1967
Department of External Affairs,
Ottawa

Kenneth Lochhead

I like to paint.

I like to look at paintings that
 reflect man's conviction, his
 grace, his sensuousness, his play,
 his delight, his creativeness, his
 coherence, his nobility, his spirit,
 and his feeling.

I believe in the celebration of life.
 Through painting I find some love
 and joy.

It is all worthwhile.

Of all the Regina painters, Lochhead was most affected by the summer Clement Greenberg spent at the Emma Lake workshop. *The Dignitary,* 1953 (ill. p. 101), is typical of the extremely competent pseudo-surrealist style he had been using to make satirical comments about the society in which he lived. Afterwards, and until 1970, he turned to hard-edge colour-field painting, staining his unsized canvases with translucent acrylic colour in disciplined, often geometric, shapes. He became, after Jack Bush, perhaps the best practitioner of this style in Canada, his compositions carefully calculated, the results taut with premeditated tensions arising from the relationships among the shapes and between the shapes and the empty canvas (ill. p. 102).

Now he has gone on past this style, abandoning the controlled approach for a much freer, more spontaneous and romantic type of painting. To admirers of Lochhead, his most recent exhibition in Toronto at the Dunkelman Gallery was a complete surprise. He had sought the aid of the airbrush to create soft fields of evanescent, steamy colour. Whereas his work of the sixties had engaged the mind as well as the feelings, he now seemed to want the viewer to turn off the critical faculties and turn on to pure, primitive, sensuous delight. In *Inner Release* (ill. p. 104), spermatozoan shapes swim in a warm sea of luminous vapour, as though all that mattered were the Eternal Now.

And yet the latest development in Lochhead's work is in the same lineage as his post-Greenberg hard-edge painting. Colour is still both form and subject. It is only that now the taut bands of colour have snapped and are drifting, half-dissolved, on the surface of the picture.

In a way, the Greenberg doctrine that colour was its own form with its own organic life must have come as a great liberating revelation to Lochhead: born in Ottawa, he studied art first (1945-9) at the Pennsylvania Academy in Philadelphia where, in the old academic way, he was taught to draw first and then to colour in the drawings. The form created by careful draughtsmanship was all-important. Colour as a separate entity was added. (In contrast Greenberg suggested that form and colour were one.) Lochhead enrolled, simultaneously with his work at the Academy, at the Barnes Foundation in Merion, Pennsylvania, famous for its collection of Matisse paintings. Lochhead claims Matisse to be the major painter of this century, and it is not hard to trace the links from this great French master of sensuous colour through the American abstract expressionists to the American colour-field painters such as Morris Louis, Helen Frankenthaler and Jules Olitski, of whom Lochhead later became aware, to Lochhead himself.

During his years of study, Lochhead also travelled in Europe and North America, studying the art collections of many museums; in 1950, he took his first teaching post, at Carleton University in Ottawa, where he was responsible for introducing studio courses in drawing and painting.

After only a year, and at the precocious age of twenty-four, he was appointed Director of the new School of Art at Regina College, University of Saskatchewan. He was not only to set up the school but to administer the Norman Mackenzie art collection, which had been left to the university and which later developed into the Norman Mackenzie Art Gallery. This was the gallery of which Ronald Bloore was to become director in 1958.

Lochhead counts the experience of setting up the art school and administering the art collection a great privilege, and crucial to his early development. He also considers that he only started to paint seriously at this time. This circumstance undoubtedly led to a lively appreciation of the artistic isolation of Regina, and the need for ideas and stimulus from outside. Thus the Emma Lake workshops. They began as summer workshops of the art school, set up as credit courses for interested art teachers. But in time and for selfish reasons, according to Lochhead, the serious artists who were involved decided to bring in people of the highest calibre to take seminars.

With a rather touching naïveté, they chose the people they invited from pictures they liked in art magazines. And yet the response itself was a form of sortation: the invited artists almost exclusively represented that aspect of American painting later known as Post-Painterly abstraction, a group label that includes a wide range of styles united by a complete acceptance of the primacy of colour.

Greenberg, when he came in 1962, was the theorist and the evangelist of the doctrine, and to the provincial artists what he had to say was nothing short of revolutionary. Lochhead says now, "There are very few people who look close at art, and Greenberg had done that and had a lot to say. . . . Although he taught us that the best and the worst were in New York, there was a lot we could do in our own environment." As for Greenberg, after his summer at Emma Lake he wrote, "I find something wonderful going on in Regina art." He listed Bloore (pages 81-8), Lochhead, Ted Godwin (pages 153-60), Arthur McKay and Douglas Morton as the Regina Five and added "Every one of these painters is more or less what I would call a 'big attack' artist." Of Lochhead in particular, he said, "He has broken through to pure flat colour stated in shapes that approach 'geometry' without really touching it. This new direction relates to nothing else in contemporary Canadian painting. . . ."

Lochhead had been exhibiting in major shows across the country since 1953, but by the sixties he was showing in international exhibitions, as, for example, *Post-Painterly Abstraction,* selected by Greenberg for the Los Angeles County

Museum in 1964. He was also included in *Canada 101,* an exhibition at the Edinburgh Festival in 1968. And he has won a number of mural commissions, including those for Gander International Airport, York University, Toronto, and the Canadian Chancery Building in Warsaw. His well-integrated mural for Winters College, York University (ill. p. 103), is one of the most successful adaptations of the artist's image to architectural décor in Canada. The painter, responding to the architectural scale, has transformed the environment with his painter's forms, lending an air of unexpected and irrational magic in a way well beyond the usual decorative appliqué one has come to expect.

Since 1964 Lochhead has been teaching at the School of Art, University of Manitoba, Winnipeg. Slim and rangy, with an outgoing personality and an obvious appetite for life, he looks much younger than his forty-five years. He talks readily and easily, making his points even in private conversation as though he were in the classroom. While prepared to admit that geography may have some effect on the nature of a region's painting, he is strongly of the opinion that art knows no boundaries and is universal (a word he prefers to "international" which, in common with many other Canadian artists, he feels connotes mere fashion and the superficial influence of the popular media).

The thing he emphasizes when discussing the profound influence of the American painters and the critic Greenberg who came to Emma Lake is their sense of commitment. And, a strong individualist, he is not afraid to voice an unpopular elitism, a belief in the value of "high art" as opposed to the "art to the people" movement: "What we lack in Canada today," he says, "is highly developed, strong-minded individuals who believe in the importance of individual effort."

He obviously believes that art history, if not all history, is the story of strong men and not of strong movements.

Kenneth Lochhead
The Dignitary
oil on canvas
16'' x 30¼''   1953
National Gallery of Canada,
Ottawa

Kenneth Lochhead
Dark Green Centre
acrylic on canvas
82'' x 80''   1963
Art Gallery of Ontario
(Gift from the McLean Foundation, 1965),
Toronto

Kenneth Lochhead
York University Mural (Untitled)
liquid polymer emulsion on canvas on plywood
144″ x 144″   1967
York University,
Toronto

Kenneth Lochhead
Inner Release
acrylic on canvas
46¹/₂″ x 42″   1971
Jack Orr Collection,
Toronto

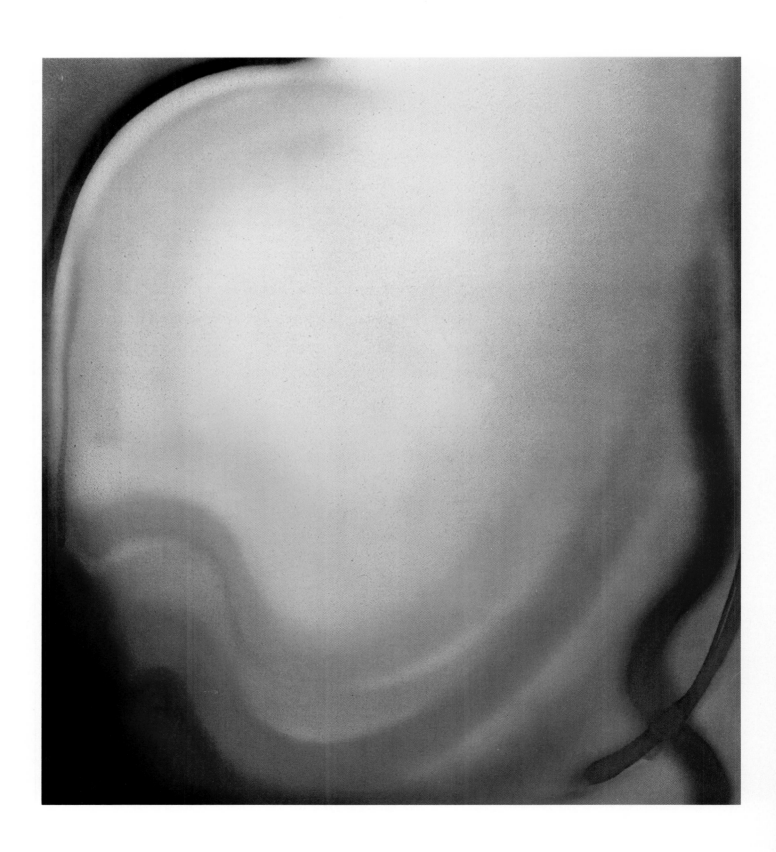

William Ronald

About painting — you only learn about it from looking at it and doing it. I don't know any other way. The greatest power of art is that it teaches you how to see. The tragedy of art is that most artists spend their lives involved with refinement. There's no sense of development.

The true painter has a strong image of himself — the degree of freedom, self-determination, and controlled spontaneity that one has is governed by the level of this image. Image is not ego — I can't describe it any better. I simply know you have to have it.

William Ronald is a self-styled "personality": an articulate, aggressive showman who has latterly combined a successful Canadian television career with his art. He gives the impression, especially at public functions, of being twice as large as he is by virtue of a commanding head and a powerful stage presence. In the late fifties and early sixties, though, when he was painting full time and full-out, he was undoubtedly one of Canada's best abstract expressionist painters. He was also one of the first of his generation to gain a reputation outside Canada, and the very first Canadian modernist to be taken on by a major dealer, the Kootz Gallery, in New York. Earlier, he had been a key figure in the Painters Eleven story.

Like his brother, John Meredith (pages 145-52), William Ronald has dropped his surname, Smith, in favour of his two given names. He was born in Stratford, Ontario, of an English father and a French-Canadian mother, whom he thinks to have had some Canadian Indian blood.

The family was poor. His father was a market gardener, but he was a sympathetic and liberal parent — and he had a drawing talent; he used to do black and white sketches of schooners. There was an uncle who drew caricatures, and an aunt who was a professional musician. One of his grandfathers was a blacksmith and the other a carpenter, so that the two boys grew up to be capable with their hands. These details are not unimportant, for this was a family that produced not one but two good painters. Ronald says that his mother's side of the family was "emotionally" French, and included some amateur performers. It is to this side that Ronald attributes his own interest in broadcasting and showbusiness.

Ronald became interested in art when he was still in public school in Stratford, and by the age of twelve he recalls seriously trying to become an artist, setting himself to copying pictures with great dedication. At eighteen he went to work in a war plant, learning to run various sorts of lathes and shapers. Two years later he had a job as "efficiency expert" on the team producing Canada's first jet plane.

In 1947 he enrolled at the Ontario College of Art. The emphasis was on techniques and discipline and every artist who went through the o.c.a. experience during those years tells the story differently. Ronald's memories are essentially negative. He has commented (in *Canadian Art*, November/December 1965), "I had worked for three years in a factory to earn the money to go there and all those debs made me sick. The only teacher there who saw anything in my work was Jock Macdonald. In third year I was told I had no right to be there because of a water colour I'd done. Macdonald calmed the situation down. Before I finished my fourth year I had already been accepted in exhibitions, so they graduated me with first class honours. But if I'd listened to them I'd be nothing today."

Nonetheless he admits that the grounding in technique was essential, saying that an artist also can teach himself but that either way he must learn his craft.

On his graduation, in 1952, Ronald worked for a year at the Robert Simpson Company in Toronto as a display artist.

In 1962 he took six weeks off, at the urging of Jock Macdonald, and went to New York to study with the artist Hans Hofmann, who was running his own painting classes. Ronald recalls that Hofmann never criticized his work because by that time he [Ronald] was "too advanced" but nonetheless says he learned a great deal from watching Hofmann run his classes. He ranks Hofmann and Jock Macdonald as "the two greatest teachers of the century."

It was after his return to Toronto that Painters Eleven had its genesis, and Ronald is justly proud of his crucial role. He was painting steadily at the time but, in common with all the other abstract artists in English Canada, was finding it almost impossible to get his work shown. Then, through his connection with the Robert Simpson Company, he managed to persuade the company to sponsor an in-store exhibition of abstract and non-figurative art. Called *Abstracts at Home*, the exhibition presented the work of seven abstract artists hung in room settings. The chosen artists were Jack Bush (pages 49-56), Kazuo Nakamura, Tom Hodgson, Ray Mead, Alexandra Luke, Oscar Cahen and Ronald himself. Ronald's paintings were hung in a Danish modern décor. Few of the seven had known each other prior to the event. They had little in common except an anti-establishment attitude and they subscribed to no joint manifesto. But, because of the success of the show, Painters Eleven was born. With four other like-minded painters, they joined forces to get more showings for their work and showed together for a number of years until the centripetal force of their disparate styles, approaches and philosophies broke up the group. But even before they disbanded Ronald had quit them, in ethical disagreement with their willing involvement with an "establishment" gallery.

In any case, he was going to New York. His work had already attracted attention there (with the bias towards abstract expressionism there, Painters Eleven was invited in 1956 to exhibit at the annual American Abstract Painters Exhibition and did so, to critical acclaim), and after a year the aggressive, influential Kootz Gallery put him under contract. (Kootz at the time also handled Hans Hofmann). When Ronald moved to New York he was twenty-nine. His work was vaguely cubistic, but with an overall lyricism and freedom that was attractive, if scarcely special. Ronald estimates that at the time there were at least a thousand abstract artists in New York as good as he was.

The Kootz contract was virtually an indenture: it required at least eighteen paintings a year at a fixed fee. Ronald lived on 2nd Avenue and, while his wife worked, painted full time. Under the whip of the Kootz contract he moved from his former style to a dense, powerful central form built up with angry, gestural strokes which piled masses of pigment on the canvas in large jagged areas (ill. p. 110). Ronald has said, "Painting, you are at war. The ones that make it as art are the ones you defeat."

Most of his buyers were New Yorkers. Those few paintings sold in Canada were purchased by Canadians who went down to New York rather than buy from Canadian sources. In a survey conducted by *Time* magazine in the late fifties, it was found that, of 250,000 painters trying to make a living from working full time at their art, only forty succeeded. Ronald was one of the forty. And he was doing, to echo the critic Dennis Reid, "his best work."

But, when his contract with the Kootz Gallery expired, Ronald found he was, under the pressure of eighteen paintings a year, "painted out."

In 1964 he returned to Toronto for a break, and went to live on Ward's Island in Toronto Bay. The quasi-rural life soon rejuvenated him and while he was there he painted an unique mural in the interior of a rectory connected to an Anglican church on the island. Unfortunately the city took over the Toronto islands for parkland, the rectory has been left vacant and the mural, though given by Ronald to the city, has been allowed to deteriorate.

This same year he began his "Umbrella" show on CBC-TV and did no painting. He has been a television star and broadcasting personality ever since. He lives now with his family in a middle-class district not far from Markham Village in Toronto, and is painting steadily. His contemporary image combines some of the poetry of his earlier work with the strong colours of his abstract expressionist phase, united in controlled, undulating rhythms of flat opaque colour.

He now sells his paintings without the benefit of a gallery or a dealer. These benefits, he claims, are not only questionable but in his case unnecessary, for he is now making "three times as much money" as he ever did.

William Ronald
In Dawn the Heart
oil on canvas
72¹/₈'' x 39⁷/₈''   1954
Art Gallery of Ontario
(Gift from J. S. McLean,
Canadian Fund, 1955),
Toronto

William Ronald
J'Accuse
oil on canvas
60'' x 69''   1956
Robert McLaughlin Gallery,
Oshawa, Ontario

William Ronald
Barbara's 1st Tantric
acrylic on cotton
120" x 168"   1968
Collection of the artist

William Ronald
Ontario Place
oil on cotton
78″ x 60″ 1971
Collection of the artist

Michael Snow

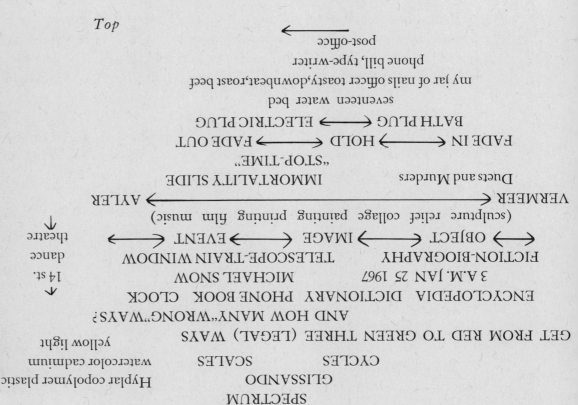

The above was written in Dec. 1966
in New York for an exhibition at the Vancouver
Art Gallery (from Jan. 5 to 29, 1967).
Now (3.00 p.m. March 26, 1970),
rereading it at the National Gallery of Canada
in Ottawa it still seems relevant. Later . . . .

THE BODY OF ALBERT AYLER, THE GREAT BLACK AMERICAN TENOR SAXOPHONIST, WAS FOUND IN THE HUDSON RIVER, NEW YORK, IN DECEMBER 1970. IT IS NOT KNOWN WHETHER HIS DEATH WAS AN ACCIDENT, SUICIDE OR MURDER. HE WAS 34 YEARS OLD.

9.00 a.m. JANUARY 9, 1974
JAMES BAY!
THIS TEXT WAS WRITTEN BY MICHAEL SNOW

THIS TEXT WAS WRITTEN JAN. 1972 BY MICHAEL SNOW TO BE ADDED TO THE ABOVE STATEMENTS WHICH WERE PRINTED ON THE CATALOGUE FOR HIS EXHIBITION AT THE XXXVth VENICE BIENNALE, SUMMER 1970. (HE REPRESENTED CANADA.)

In surveying and evaluating the work of Michael Snow, it is necessary to go beyond his painting. While it is true that others in this book have worked outside of the field of paint-on-canvas, Snow is unique in that painting has never been his true art, but only a part of it: Snow's concern has been with probing for answers to the nature of visual reality; painting is one method among many of approaching the problem.

Even for the initiated, Snow's work if often difficult. He is a true child of the McLuhan age: fascinated with cybernetics, viewing the world as a "system" loaded with many-level interlocking meanings, given to complex puns and allusions, he transposes McLuhanism from words to images.

His acute and almost painful perception of his environment constitutes his "subject matter"; his insights can be triggered by the detritus of everyday living, as in *Press, 1969*, a work in which he pressed cigarettes, rubber gloves, and dead fish between plates of glass and photographed them like some kind of obsessive archivist of our disintegrating ecology.

Although Snow's McLuhanist vision makes him the antithesis of the regional artist, his background is the essence of Canadianism: he was born, in 1929, in Toronto, his father of English origin and United Empire Loyalist background, his mother a French-Canadian native of Chicoutimi, Quebec. He lived at various times in Montreal, Toronto, Chicoutimi and Winnipeg; his schooling included Upper Canada College and the Ontario College of Art, where he graduated from the Design Course. "Totally uncertain" of what his interests were, Snow's work showed the influences of Klee, Matisse and Mondrian as well as of the various modern schools of European painting; even for a student, Snow was remarkably eclectic. His need to search out new grounds — a delineation of the framework for his experiments — led him to music (he was a pianist with the famous Toronto Mike White Imperial Jazz Band) and then to film as an animator for the short-lived Graphic Films company. At Graphic he met the artist Joyce Wieland (pages 121-8), whom he subsequently married.

During the fifties in Toronto the thought of making a living from art was ridiculous and jobs as musician and film-maker helped him survive financially; later they were to give a distinctive shape to his art.

When not at work making a living, Snow was painting; he appears to have been entirely oblivious to the various Canadian movements then springing up: the Emma Lake Workshops or the Automatistes. Even today he is more interested, and well versed, in international than in Canadian art history.

He did, however, join the lively group of young painters who exhibited at the newly established Isaacs Gallery, where he had his first one-man show in 1957. This followed by a year a showing at Hart House and it is easy to recall, nearly twenty years later, the excitement and sense of discovery of that exhibit.

At times Snow has been prophetic; his 1960 painting *Lac Clair* (ill. p. 117) was greeted with derision at that time but in fact it stands as an intriguing example of the colour-field school of painting when almost no one in Toronto was aware of the movement going on in New York.

In 1962, the Snows emigrated to New York where, at times, his work anticipated the exciting art of that school, but he almost completely rejected the mammoth scale of the New York painters as being unsuitable for his concepts. Perhaps because of that, it was not until he returned to his old interest in film that he was acclaimed as a star in the international firmament of the arts. However, it would be inaccurate and unjust to suggest that he lacked an appreciative following as a painter: in 1964, 1965 and 1968 he was given successful one-man shows at the respected Poindexter Gallery in New York.

Finally, in 1971, while protesting no particular national patriotism (unlike his wife), Snow and Wieland returned to Toronto; he feels now that his presence in this country as a working artist is a positive contribution towards preserving what is worthwhile in Canada. It is worth noting that this conviction is true, despite the fact that his art continues to be undeniably international in vocabulary.

In 1959, shortly before Snow left Canada, he set for himself an almost incredible discipline, one he came on by accident: working on a collage, he cut out the figure of a walking woman, which he intended to use as a stencil. But the shape presented a challenge to Snow, a new vehicle through which he could continue his absorbing quest for answers to visual reality; for ten years, working almost solely within the self-imposed limits of the woman's figure, he played every conceivable change and variation on this theme. The *Walking Woman* appeared in repeatables (a manifestation of Snow's fascination with film), a line of silver sculptured figures at the entrance to the Ontario Pavilion at Expo 67 (mirroring the crowds who passed by and acting as a graphic symbol, leading them to the pavilion). She walked toward the left and the right edges of canvases, she was monocoloured and multicoloured, she faced in both directions and at various levels, various heights and various depths (*Venus Simultaneous*, ill. p. 118), she was printed on T-shirts worn by Snow's friends; she appeared on 42nd Street in New York, on the Toronto subway and at several airport terminals. A lifesize figure in profile, her arms swinging smartly, she was eventually used in a Coke advertisement, an especially fitting context: the *Walking Woman* is a comment on the simultaneity of international visual experience, of which the Coke bottle is a leading example.

Further, the repetition of the woman and the places in which she turned up were consistent with Snow's perception of art as taking place in life — both "out there" in the world, a part, though not categorically a part of it.

Robert Fulford, writing in 1970 in *Michael Snow, a Survey,* calls the development of the *Walking Woman,* "perhaps the single most important event in Canadian art since Borduas." He continues, "Given a smaller talent than Snow's [it] could have produced nothing more than a series of parodies — and possibly at times parody was involved, but, although the gap between parody and high art is fairly large Snow spanned it easily. His work in this period became the most satisfying in his career that far, partly because he had this icon, this image, this jumping-off point, to rely on. Freed of the necessity to invent the basic form for each work of art, Snow concentrated his intellectual energy on what has always mattered most in his art — the process of creation itself."

In 1961 Snow spoke of himself in terms that are most applicable to his art as a whole: "I make up the rules of the game and attempt to play it. If I seem to be losing, I change the rules." This pragmatic approach extricated him from what even some of his admirers feared for a time was a trap: he appeared to have wrung all the changes from the *Walking Woman* game and the art community watched expectantly for a new game to be invented. Without losing stride, Snow invented several new ones and moved into other media with ever-increasing power and invention. It may have been that he had been suppressing ideas in conforming to the demands of the *Woman,* but these ideas had not been dissipated; they had simply been simmering, waiting their time.

Dennis Young, former curator of contemporary art at the Art Gallery of Ontario and the man who organized the 1970 retrospective, says in the catalogue: ". . . the line from [Marcel] Duchamp cannot be overemphasized; Snow is among the very few on whom the mantle of Duchamp descends appropriately." Like Duchamp, Snow pursues his witty, iconoclastic, but profound, search for definitions of art. Snow's preoccupation with framing, evident in so much of his work, is richly symbolic of the artist who keeps seeking the limits (or framework) of art and who is constantly testing himself against those limits, not out of a sense of rebellion or hostility but as the compulsive exploration of a first-rate intellect. Snow is unquestionably a leading Canadian painter during a great flowering of Canadian painting; nonetheless his international reputation today is founded on his films. In fact, many European cinéastes, who revere Snow's work, are surprised to find that he is "also" a painter of excellent reputation.

Michael Snow's continual absorption with the questions of "what is Art/what is reality/what is their relationship?" probably has no definable end, no moment when he can say with satisfaction "I have all the answers" and put aside his work. As Robert Fulford has said, "Almost everything written about Snow becomes quickly obsolete." However frustrating that may be for the author trying to pin Snow to paper, it is a significant index of his richness as an artist.

Michael Snow
Lac Clair
oil & paper on canvas
70″ x 70″   1960
National Gallery of Canada,
Ottawa

Michael Snow
Red Square
oil on canvas
42″ x 50″   1960
Toronto-Dominion Bank,
Toronto

Michael Snow
Venus Simultaneous
oil on canvas & wood
79'' x 118''   1962
Art Gallery of Ontario,
Toronto

Michael Snow
Switch
oil on canvas
60" x 45"   1963
Robert Fulford Collection,
Toronto

Joyce Wieland

The older I get the more I feel it is an honour to be an artist.

Although I have taken lots of years of suffering and labour to become a good artist, it is not for me like holding some great reward. . . . I want to share it and keep on becoming a better artist and at the same time help people understand art.

As for my own art . . . Canada is my iconography and has been for some time . . . and as far as I can see in the future will continue to be so. I am interested in so many aspects, legends like Tom Thompson, the landscape, etc., that I want to make into films and painting.

I want to say something about nationalism by serving my country as an artist.

In Joyce Wieland two important artistic facets have been fused to make her the most important female artist in Canada today: Wieland has talent and she has something to say. Despite the fact that she has not used paint on canvas for several years, she remains worthy of considerable attention.

Wieland's colour sense, her ability to use it with expressive power, is built on her solid foundation as an expert draughtsman. Her freedom to use paint naturally is evident in *Nature Mixes* (ill. p. 127), where a flower turns to a penis turns to a flower turns to a hand turns to a flower. In the process the paint seems almost to become the object. Like her husband, Michael Snow (pages 113-20), Wieland has been influenced by film and this influence is easy to trace in the repeated frames of *Nature Mixes* and also in *Sail Boat Sinks* (ill. p. 128). In fact, she still returns to film as an important means of expression, though she claims she first used it to escape from the influence of her husband's work. *Sail Boat Sinks* also pinpoints another aspect of Wieland's character: her artistic preoccupation with accidents. (They are always accidents which are expressed in various types of plane crashes and boat collisions or sinkings.) Like a lot of our most talented artists, in many fields, Wieland is obsessed with time and with the fact that it is short, too short to accommodate all that must be expressed. This, too, is evident in her interest in film where, unlike painting, art takes place in time as well as in space.

A short, plump woman, unmindful of her appearance, Joyce Wieland was born in Toronto, elder daughter of British immigrants. She attended Central Technical School to learn to be a commercial artist and still feels that her training there, under Carl Schaeffer, Doris McCarthy and Bob Ross, was a useful grounding for her later work. This background in commercial art may account for her present iconography, in which she makes use of popular advertising images and slogans. But her main interest during her early years as a developing artist was the human figure.

When Wieland was in her early twenties, she went to Europe "to see the museums" and, at that period in her life, decided that she wanted to become a "serious" artist. On her return to Toronto, she became a film animator at Graphic Films, where she met Michael Snow. Her career is tied into the history of the Isaacs Gallery in Toronto, which was established in a tiny shop in what was then known as Greenwich Village. Here she and Gordon Rayner (pages 177-84) shared the second exhibition to be presented. Her work in those days was semi-abstract, featuring a series of portraits of imaginary people; she, like several other young Toronto artists, Hedrick, Coghtry, Rayner, Markle, were fascinated for some time with the human figure in space and she executed a series of pen drawings entitled *Flying Lovers*.

While she became aware of the abstract expressionist movement dominating New York during the 1950s, Wieland continued this interest in the human body, as well as in a study of cubism and historical portraiture, especially as found in early German art.

In 1961, she made some abstract paintings and wooden collages mixed with pieces of cloth. She called these pieces *The Clothes of Love*. Influenced by her sister, who is a quiltmaker, Wieland became interested in the use of cloth as an art form, but these first works were not sewn; later she produced her first quilts. Her aim was to get quiltmakers, particularly her sister, involved in the creative process in which she herself was caught up. She was particularly intrigued with the idea of making art specifically for people: designing costumes of quilts based on the more hidden characteristics of some of her friends. The first important piece of this kind was a small quilt she designed for the son of a friend, built around his personality.

Like her husband, whose *Walking Woman* turned up in various countries, Wieland was fascinated with "traveling art" and the quilt actually travelled when the family for whom it was made journeyed around the world.

From these early works, Wieland felt challenged to raise the quilt from being a handicraft to becoming a high art form.

In 1963, she and Snow went to live in New York, though she was reluctant to go. However, the move gave her a new perspective on Canada: she saw, first, that her exhibitions and her sales were still largely Canadian and this, in turn, led her to consider Canada as a subject for her art. Perhaps earlier than most of us, she began to be concerned about what lay ahead for this country and she started a still unfinished quilt on the subject of General Wolfe. This was followed by other works dealing specifically with the subject of the problematic future of Canada: *The Freedom Quilt, J'Aime Le Canada* and *Down with U.S. Imperialism*.

In New York she and Snow experienced first hand the freewheeling "bohemian" life, living and working in a grimy loft in lower Manhattan. This vantage point helped Wieland look at Canada from a new perspective and she became intensely political in her art.

In 1970, certain that New York had become a decadent place for artists to work and that the "good old days" of abstract expressionism, when New York was the artistic mecca of the world, were over, the Snows returned to Canada.

Wieland's life-style is in transition at the moment because of the change from the New York loft to this country. She and her husband have always had a little log house in the Maritimes, and they now have a house in Toronto. She does not teach, feeling that her artistic energies should be devoted full time to doing things for her country in order to heighten the consciousness of the Canadian people. Her immediate project is a film on Canada, dealing with the Tom Thomson myth.

Critics have often described Wieland's work as satirical; in fact, she was represented in an exhibition called *The Satirical in Art* at York University in 1966, but her artistic commentary on our packaged pop culture is highly individual and she is not part of the satirical wing of the pop art movement. In commenting on her recent retrospective at the National Gallery, Ottawa, in the summer of 1971, she emphasized that she wished to avoid any irony or satire, hoping instead to create an exhibit of exclusively positive works. She sees herself as not political so much as patriotic and of her work she says: "Good God, look at this place; good God, look at these legends I am making up from what I have found out about Canada." Indeed, her aim for the past two years has been to create works which are, in her words, "as beautiful and inspiring as I could make them." Speaking of the *True Patriot Love* show at the National Gallery, Hugo MacPherson said (*artscanada* review, August-September 1971), "Wieland sees a myth (i.e. Canada) that could become a reality."

Though no artist should be limited by labels, it is reasonable to place Wieland as a pop artist; like Andy Warhol, who shares the pop label, Wieland believes in democratizing art: at the Ottawa exhibit she involved many people – artists, non-artists – in the production of objects which were exhibited. This doesn't mean that she encourages amateurism, but that she wishes to blur the demarcation line between crafts and high art, as she has done so successfully with the quilts. In one of her latest projects she hopes to involve hundreds of people in *her* art production and through them create a quilt of parts made in all the provinces of Canada. This astonishing piece of proposed participatory needlework, when put together, would be more than six hundred feet long! This is one more evidence of her love of Canada; in her own words: "I have so much to claim."

Joyce Wieland
Hallucination
oil & collage
76'' x 102''   1961
The Isaacs Gallery Collection,
Toronto

Joyce Wieland
Time Machine Series
oil on canvas
80″ x 106¼″ 1961
Art Gallery of Ontario
(Gift from the McLean Foundation, 1966),
Toronto

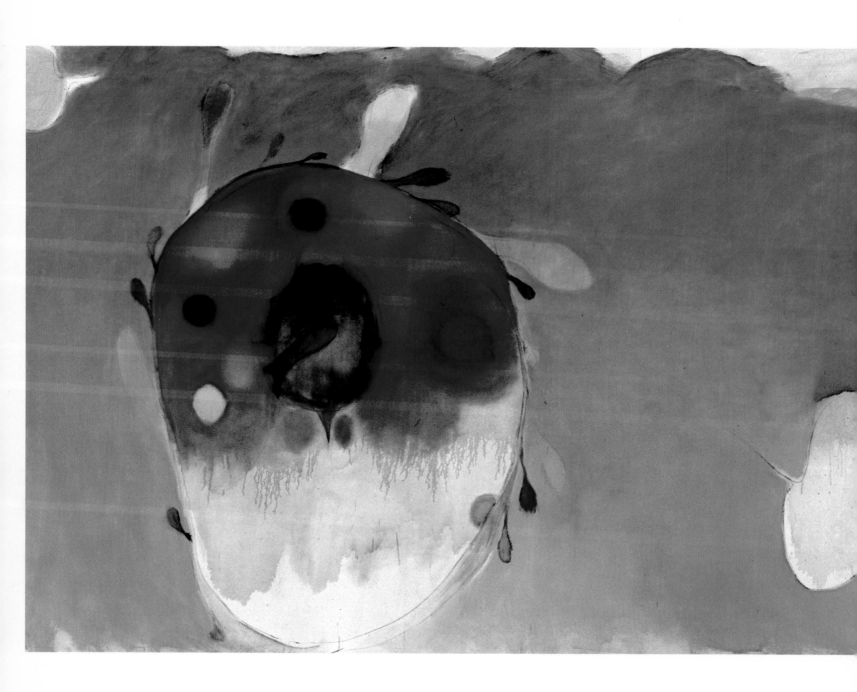

Joyce Wieland
Nature Mixes
oil on canvas
12" x 16"   1963
Mr. Udo Kasements Collection,
Toronto

Joyce Wieland
Boat Tragedy
oil on canvas
20″ x 48″   1964
Art Gallery of Ontario
(Gift from the Toronto-
Dominion Bank, 1965),
Toronto

Jack Chambers

I am not interested in art, I am interested in life. When you are interested in life more than you are in painting, then your paintings can come to life. This is perceptual realism where life is a motivating force.... Perceptual Realism ... Perceptualism, to make it brief, starts from objective reality ... a tree looks like a tree.

You have in the completed painting an integrated unity ... an integrated focus of intention at work here ... which people in their own lives grope for and have a deep longing for when they turn to life itself, to their own lives, for meaning and focus. They try to understand their wordly life as they exist in it and as they are working in it, in a unified way, so that a particle of life, any particle, can be looked at and the complete meaning can be seen without having to see the whole. The whole can be envisioned by understanding the particle. What I am trying to get at with Perceptualism is that at first you start from objective realism ... accepting the world as it is.

Then the painting has this 'infusion', this ... the unified spirit in it, which is the parallel to the kind of spirit which is also in the world. We cannot often find or see it. The painting turns out to be, in a way, a 'jolt' to our unconscious memories of the completeness we want to have, and intuitively know is there, and may never have been able to encounter.

When you parallel this with perceptualism, you get the kind of intention I am after. The work itself is to provide a vision ... a vision seen behind the paradox of reality of the everyday mundane. You have to repeat that 'everyday' so exactly that the intention within it becomes the vision you see and you do not get stuck on the surface.

It could be a few days before Christmas and the two little boys in pyjamas and bathrobes sit in the greenish-yellow morning light, watching television intently. It's Sunday in a London, Ontario, suburb and the children are waiting patiently for their parents to awaken. The picture is one of contentment: the youngsters warm in their Doctor Dentons, their teddy-bears lying easily on the floor, the snow clear and crisp outside the picture window. This is surely the best-known, most often reproduced vignette of a casual weekend morning in Canada: though it was completed only two years ago, it is the already famous subject of Jack Chambers' four foot square *Sunday Morning #2* (ill. p. 134).

Sunday Morning #2 is a measure of its creator's daring and his excellence: going against the flow of art three years ago, he committed himself to realism, without the additional surrealist vocabulary he had used until then; the work was successful both in commercial and artistic terms and has had a considerable effect on Canadian painting. For while Alex Colville (pages 57-64) has continued to work in his meticulous and honest way, and has influenced a small but distinct group, mostly of his own students, his power has almost never extended beyond that circle. Chambers, however, though not himself a teacher, has had a farther ranging, though less direct, effect on painters, some of whom are now involved in realism. His accomplishment has confirmed for older artists the value of figurative painting and has shown younger ones that realism is a professionally acceptable style. Chambers, like Colville, has made it clear that realism is not the last resort of the unimaginative, but, in the hands of the gifted artist, can have an arresting, almost religious quality that is uniquely moving.

The apparent matter-of-fact sunniness of *Sunday Morning #2* would seem a logical work for a handsome young painter from one of the richest, most conservative cities in Canada; but Chambers' work is informed with greater depth and more poignance, perhaps because the road from London to *Sunday Morning #2* has been filled with experimentation, with detours and with tortuous artistic risk. A co-operative retrospective by the Vancouver Art Gallery and the Art Gallery of Ontario, mounted in 1970, documents Chambers' growth from his beginnings as a promising student, whose sources of inspiration were evident, to his present stature as an important artist.

Jack Chambers was born in London and attended school there; he was a student at Beal Technical School, which had an art department of outstanding excellence. (In fact, almost every one of the so-called "London school" of painters went through the art classes at Beal.) But Chambers (who won his first award at the Western Ontario Art Exhibition in 1950 for "a work by an artist under the age of 27") found the atmosphere of his home city artistically stifling and decided to travel abroad. His goal at that point was not so much art as self-discovery — the kind of museum-filled tour which many artists make before committing themselves professionally. Once the decision was made, Chambers went to Europe and enrolled at the Academy of Fine Arts in Madrid, where he studied for six years; he financed these studies by winning a series of scholarships – the Elizabeth R. Greenshields Foundation Scholarship (Montreal) in 1956, the State Prize for Painting, the Royal Academy of Madrid and the Paular Scholarship for Landscape Painting, Spain, in 1958. In those years he lived in the village of Chinchon, near Madrid, and it provided the subject matter of many of his early paintings.

His first work was greatly influenced by El Greco and others of the Golden Age of Spanish painting – not surprising when one considers that these men exerted an inescapable influence on Spanish art, comparable to that of Borduas in relation to Quebec art.

Unlike other European countries, whose academies ceased to be a serious factor in art in the twentieth century, the Spanish academy has continued to flourish and to insist on a rigorously traditional and academic program of teaching. From it, Chambers has taken considerable technical discipline, evident in his work and crucial to his present "perceptual realism," his own name for his style today.

Chambers has always tried to go beneath objective reality; he seeks to interpret, to express the inner spiritual and psychic meaning of experience; the paintings which followed his graduation from the academy were strangely crude and naive attempts to work out a religious crisis he was going through at the time, as he converted from the Baptist faith to Roman Catholicism. In doing so, he temporarily turned his back on the skills that he had so rigorously developed at the academy.

Chambers returned to London in 1961 and his paintings assumed a mystical, dreamlike and very nostalgic quality, full of childhood memories that had a dimension beyond the incidents themselves; it seemed that, returning home after an extended absence spent in a totally different culture, Chambers was restructuring his past life – reorienting himself to the environment that had originally created him. In 1963, Chambers married Olga Sanchez Bustos, and she has appeared in most of his paintings since then. Until 1967, dream-like visions, from which apparitions sometimes float, haunted his canvases; in the later part of that period, the influence of movies made itself felt. In 1968, Richard Hamilton, British artist and teacher, chose *Regatta No. 1*, as the top work in the Art Gallery of Ontario exhibit, *Canadian Artists '68*. Its main panel is of a family group; a series of movie-like frames runs down the right hand side. The emphasis is a concern with the passage of time, a sad irony for Chambers who, that year, was told that he was incurably ill with leukaemia. Many stories on Chambers have emphasized this tragic aspect of his life, which is a disservice to a serious artist. The knowledge, in fact, has not changed either the man or his art, though it may have intensified certain elements of his life: his enjoyment of his wife and two children, his serious dedication to his painting, his love of nature and his deep mysticism.

Chambers' first exhibition was not in Canada, but in Madrid, at the Lorca Gallery; his first one-man show took place in 1963 at the Isaacs Gallery in Toronto and, in that same year, he was included in the National Gallery's Fifth Biennal of Canadian Paintings; since then, Chambers' work has been part of all the important exhibitions in this country. With his artist friends in London — including Curnoe (pages 185-92) — he has been active in a number of creative activities other than painting: he illustrated a book of poems by James Reaney, *Dance of Death in London,* and has had his own poetry published in Reaney's little magazine, *Alphabet*; in addition, stories and articles of his have appeared in the magazine *Region*.

Despite these incursions into literature and a continuing interest in film making, Chambers remains, first and foremost, a painter. In the late sixties, he began to find that he could make the fullest use of the rich, disciplined training he had undergone to say, in the most direct way possible, how he experienced life. He dropped the surrealist elements from his work and began to concentrate on realism; his work has a Vermeer quality (for example, the use of light and the contrast between the warm room and cold outdoors in *Sunday Morning*); his perceptual realism captures effectively his continuing concerns — light and, on the other hand, death. Chambers uses source photographs for his paintings and some of these have been reproduced in his catalogues, for example, the catalogue which accompanied the 1970 retrospective. If anything, these make clear how fine an artist Chambers is: he invests the ordinary photos with a significance of almost religious intensity, a meaning beyond the object or scene itself. On the face of it, the subject matter he chooses is parochial; his genius is to have raised the everyday to the level of universality. Long after additions have been made to *Victoria Hospital* (ill p. 136), long after *The 401 Towards London* (ill p. 133) has been torn up, long after the two children in *Sunday Morning* have grown into men, his paintings of those subjects will continue to have meaning.

Jack Chambers
401 Towards London, #1
oil on wood
72'' x 96''   1968-9
Northern & Central Gas Corporation Ltd.,
Toronto

Jack Chambers
Sunday Morning, #2
oil on wood
48″ x 48″   1969-70
Mr. & Mrs. E. A. Schwendau Collection,
London, Ontario

Jack Chambers
Victoria Hospital
oil on wood
48" x 96"   1970
Private Collection,
Canada

Jack Chambers
Lake Huron #1
oil on wood
72'' x 72''   1970-1
Nancy Poole's Studio Limited,
Toronto

Claude Tousignant

Text Anti-Text

As I started struggling to write this text, trying to elucidate the complex system of relationships and different elements that exist in my painting, and also my relationship to painters like Mondrian and Newman and the whole area of structural/colour painting, two things came to my mind.

First, a remark made by a young student who had come with a group visit to my studio; as I was trying to explain how a particular painting worked, he said, "You don't have to tell us all this! We can see it — it's quite evident, and if you'd get out of the way and stop talking, we should be able to see it much better!"

The second thing to come to my mind was what I consider one of the main goals of my work, which I first formulated in 1959 for the catalogue of the exhibition "Art Abstrait"; I called the article, "Pour une peinture évidentielle" — for a self-evident kind of painting. The idea was to purify painting to its basic physical elements, thereby bringing it into a universal field of understanding.

If I still have to "explain" my paintings, then my past work has been as good as useless; for the future, I have decided to let my paintings speak for themselves.

Claude Tousignant is a distinctive explorer in the field of colour op art, so distinctive, in fact, that few would dare follow in his footsteps. He set out to do a particular thing — to solve the problem posed by the abstract relationship of colour and form, a kind of art Tousignant himself calls structural/colour painting, and, taking the goal he has chosen, he has achieved it to near perfection. Thus, he has no need for disciples, for they can become, at best, only imitators.

Tousignant doesn't expect viewers of his work to bring with them a knowledge of art history, of psychoanalysis, music, chemistry or *anything* external to the experience. He wants them simply to understand the workings of colour and structure as a direct, automatic, physiological and unconditioned psychological experience. Tousignant says he considers that one of the main goals of his work is to create "a self-evident kind of painting. The idea was to purify painting to its basic physical elements, thereby bringing it into a universal field of understanding."

Tousignant, unlike most French-Canadian artists of the past thirty years, rejects the need to measure his work against that of Borduas — not disrespectfully, but out of a recognition that he, like Molinari (see pages 161-8), has chosen an entirely different path and that comparisons are specious. He says that Borduas, though passionately anti-clerical (see pages 25-7), was stamped by his Roman Catholicism, which led him to think in hierarchical terms, and made him "the high priest of art in Montreal." Tousignant implies that he doesn't want to be the leader of a new religion but at the same time is, with Molinari, self-consciously aware of his prominent place among Canadian artists.

There was nothing of the art world in Tousignant's background: he was born, of French-Canadian parents, in the heart of Montreal. A large, athletic and handsome man, he is still slightly shy about speaking English, despite a high degree of fluency. He doesn't remember being influenced in any particular way, but he found that he did very well at art in school. When he was about seventeen, he decided to become an artist, though he doesn't remember, looking back, that he was in any way swayed by the extremely lively Montreal art scene of that time. From 1948 to 1952 he was a pupil at the school of art attached to the Montreal Museum of Fine Art, where his teachers included Arthur Lismer, Jacques de Tonnancoeur, Louis Archembeault and Marion Scott. But perhaps the most important of them was Gordon Webber, who he felt wasn't understood by the other students, but who became his most vital source of inspiration. (In fact, it is worth noting that Webber has been generally underrated, both as an innovative artist in his own right and as a teacher of others in this country.) As a student at a school which was comparatively "academic," Tousignant's own work was, naturally enough, figurative.

In 1952, Tousignant left art school and went to Paris, where he stayed for two years — at a time when the art centre had shifted very decidedly from Paris to New York. He studied there at the Academie Ronson and at the Academie de la Cloison d'Or and was quite naturally influenced to a great degree by the Paris school style of the time — an influence that he considers in retrospect to have been negative and one which he had to overcome in order to achieve his present pure, "self-evident" style. Tousignant would seem to agree with the critics of the Paris School of the fifties when they characterize it as the "pastry school" — all surface illusion, delicious colour and seductive texture; in his own words, he regards "this whole Parisian adventure as a calamity."

Tousignant returned to Montreal where his first exhibit, at the gallery attached to La Galerie l'Echourie restaurant, was mounted in 1954. While it may seem curious for an important artist to be exhibited in a restaurant, the climate in Canada for abstract painters of that period was cool indeed. In fact, there were only two galleries in Montreal where Tousignant's work could have been considered for show and the L'Echourie restaurant was one of them. It was almost an artists' club and there Tousignant renewed his acquaintance with Molinari, who was exploring some of the same kinds of painting problems that fascinated Tousignant. In order to earn even a marginal livelihood, Tousignant worked for the city of Montreal at various jobs, including that of fireman and as a workman in the sewer system.

Tousignant, along with Molinari, who acted as director, and Robert Blair, started a small commercial gallery, La Galerie L'Actuelle, which, though it lasted only two years, served as a showcase for Tousignant, Harold Town (pages 73-80) and other important Canadian artists.

With the collapse of Galerie L'Actuelle, Tousignant exhibited at La Galerie Denise de Rue (which, as La Galerie du Siecle, went on to become an outlet for important and new kinds of Canadian art, in the same way as the Isaacs Gallery was in Toronto).

Up until 1961, he had been exploring the relationship between various geometric shapes of colour on the surface of the canvas; between then and 1963, he had reduced the shape to a square in a rectangular frame. In 1964, recognizing that New York was the centre of the art world, Tousignant packed up and left Canada with every intention of spending the rest of his life in New York. At the time of the move, he had begun to use a circular shape on a rectangular or square surface. at the same time changing his approach to colour: sometimes his paintings were of violently contrasting colours, sometimes of subtle, almost imperceptible, hues. Over a period of time, the circles in his paintings changed from plain, flat colour to become a series of concentric rings which whirled with optical vibrations. Eventually these were presented on circular shapes. Tousignant called them "Gongs," though they were nicknamed "Targets" (ill. p. 144).

Tousignant was so successful in New York that he was able to live entirely from his income as an artist; unlike other Canadians, principally Snow and Wieland (pages 113-20 and 121-8), whose paintings were more successful in Canada, even when they lived in the u.s. Tousignant's work was being bought by Americans. In 1965 he was included in an exhibit, *The Responsive Eye*, at New York's prestigious Museum of Modern Art; that show seemed to set the seal on him as an important op-colour painter, both in Canada and abroad. The idea of staying in New York was beginning to pall; it seemed that if Tousignant were going to work and sell in the u.s. with no intention of coming back to Canada, he should become an American citizen. But he shrank from that kind of final commitment and decided, instead, to return to this country.

He now lives and works in Montreal in a large, well-organized, well-lit studio, in contrast to its setting atop a dark, narrow stairway beside a store front. Tousignant doesn't teach and has gained enough recognition in this country to support himself as an artist with the assistance of some Canada Council funds.

Tousignant's work is, like his working space, orderly: taken as a whole, it can be seen in a sequence tight enough for time-lapse photography: the flat, monochromatic circle giving way to the concentric circles of many colours, then the circles, like marvellous one-celled animals of art, stretched into ellipses, then the ellipses breaking into two (*Double Quarante-deux*, ill. p. 144).

The full force of Tousignant's paintings depends to some extent on seeing them in their original size, in choosing a distance from the painting so that the magic optical games can begin. The artist has not chosen the size of his canvases arbitrarily, but has taken subtle physiological facts into account: the ellipses are shaped like dazzling miniature racetracks, forcing the eye to travel along the "straightaway" and then zoom around the tight turns at the ends. Each end of the ellipse has been an unmarked centre; today Tousignant has broken these centres off and made them into twin paintings, hung side-by-side with careful attention to the optical tensions these pairs create.

Tousignant's has been a virtuoso performance: every work stuns with its hypnotic optical force. But beneath the optics lies an intriguing paradox: rational means of particularly Gallic intensity have been employed to transfix the viewer. Tousignant blinds the eye, even as he binds it.

Claude Tousignant
Les Asperges
oil on canvas
51″ x 45″   1955
Collection of the artist

Claude Tousignant
Oscillation
cilux on canvas
51" x 46"   1956
Collection of the artist

Claude Tousignant
Gong-88
liquitex on canvas
diameter: 88''   1967
Art Gallery of Ontario,
Toronto

Claude Tousignant
Double Quarante-deux
polymer on canvas
diameter: 42″   1971
Collection of the artist

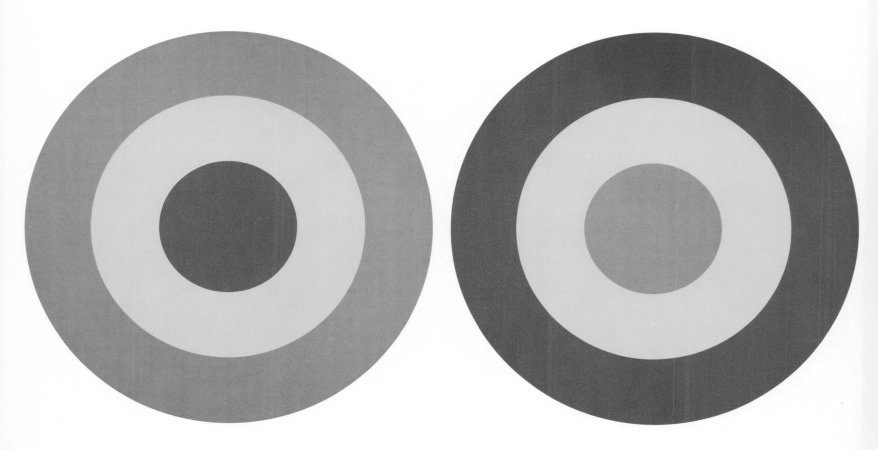

John Meredith

*Art should always be a mystery. It isn't possible to totally explain any work of
art, anyways, since it is this mysterious quality which makes art so beautiful.*

"Art," says John Meredith, "should always be a mystery. It isn't possible to totally explain any work of art anyway, since it is this mysterious quality which makes art so beautiful." It is suitable comment from an artist who uses uncomplicated techniques to create works of great originality and mystery.

Meredith's paintings are as accessible to the uninitiated viewer as they are to the most knowledgeable historian because his art is the least derivative of that included in this book and because Meredith himself has no program of explanation for it. His work is among those things that simply exist and are to be experienced. A good example is *Untitled Diptych* (ill. p. 151), the focus of which is a mandala-like form, which looks like the seal of some mystical society, surrounded by cabalistic markings. Meredith himself, however, professes little knowledge of the mandala, although it has become a popular sign in the counter-culture, with its Oriental and philosophical connotations and its Jungian application as symbolic of the effort to reunify the self. But Meredith has come to it less intellectually, more instinctively, and shows little interest in investing his work with meanings borrowed from other spheres of human thought or activity. This attitude is as true of his other works; Meredith paints from his viscera, not from his head.

This may help explain why he has remained singularly uninfluenced by the work of other Canadian artists, an astonishing fact when one considers that he is the younger brother of William Ronald (pages 105-12), a man who was a mover and maker in Painters Eleven and in the artistic revolution which shook Toronto in the late fifties.

John Meredith was born in 1933 in the town of Fergus, Ontario, and was interested in drawing and painting by the time he was in grade three. He left school as a youngster and went to work in an aircraft factory; in 1950, with the blessing of sympathetic parents, he enrolled in the Ontario College of Art in Toronto, where he studied until 1953. His teachers included Carl Schaeffer, Eric Freifeld and, most important, Jock Macdonald (pages 17-24), who encouraged him to go his own way artistically. Although he has a solid grounding in drawing the human figure (the core of the o.c.a. curriculum at that time) and feels that such a background is useful to any artist, he showed little interest in it.

During his years at the college, when his brother, William Ronald was becoming a highly articulate leading figure of the Toronto art scene, Meredith pursued his own lifestyle, living in Brampton and commuting to Toronto for classes. He had little social contact with Painters Eleven, a group he considers to have been in the generation before his own; by the time Meredith began to exhibit, Painters Eleven had disbanded. Both brothers have dropped the family name, Smith, and each uses his given names only, for professional reasons.

Meredith believes that, if he has been influenced at all, it is by Borduas and Les Automatistes and even that was not a stylistic influence but rather brought about a change in attitude, a kind of release that helped him find his own personal language of expression.

His first exhibition, in 1958, was at the Gallery of Contemporary Art in Toronto; two years later he joined the group, jocularly known as Isaacs' Allstars, who show at the Isaacs Gallery. He has had five one-man shows at the Isaacs since 1961.

In the years since then, he has been included, in Canada, in the National Gallery's Biennial (1965), and in every major survey show mounted to the present day; internationally, he has been represented in a group show at Buffalo's Albright Knox Gallery (1963-64), the International Biennial in Paris (1965), the Gallery of Modern Art, Paris (1967), the *Nine Canadians* show at the Institute of Contemporary Art in Boston (1968), *Canada 101* in Edinburgh in the same year and in the Tenth International *Black and White Exhibition* in Lugano (1968) and *Eight Artists from Canada* in Tel Aviv (1971).

Meredith regards 1962 as particularly important in his artistic evolution; in that year he produced *Bengal* (ill. p. 149) which, to his mind, is a key work. In it he transferred a drawing technique to painting; the blurring of the ink line which was to become his unique trademark intrigued him for some years and in *Bengal* he moved it for the first time from drawing to painting. From 1964 on it became his signature.

Meredith's technique is painstaking and of great interest: he does his work first in the form of small drawings, which he has collected over the past fifteen years; he selects one of these and then enlarges it (his canvases often exceed eight feet in size) almost without change in what he calls the most "traditional manner possible," graphing the small sketch and the large canvas. This method releases him from the problem of form so that he can throw all his energies into the challenge of colour. The astonishing and delightful mystery of his work is that, despite its meticulousness, it has the spontaneity and excitement of art created in a single burst of inspiration.

Meredith's unique imagery *is* spontaneous and comes purely from his unconscious. Because his work is perhaps the most original of that of any Canadian artist, critics have pressed him to discuss its origins. In an interview with Barry Lord of the National Gallery of Canada, he finally protested: "don't try to explain it all away." He does, however, say that the style which has grown out of his pen and ink sketches lends movement to his paintings; although this style was initially uncalculated, its artistic exploitation continues to give him pleasure. What he does with these forms is not accidental; the inspiration may be seemingly non-intellectual, but the manipulation of them on the surface of the canvas is directed by a keen visual mind.

Meredith has remained a loner. In the days when Isaacs' Allstars made the nearby Pilot Tavern the scene of endless talk and argument about art, Meredith continued to live in Brampton, staying there till 1964. He now lives completely as an artist, making his home in his studio, a large single room over a store on Toronto's Spadina Avenue, near the garment district. Quiet and shy, hesitant in articulating his ideas, he has never taught and never been active in the art associations that continually mushroom. Although he lives a relatively isolated life, Meredith has no sense of rejection, having built up over the past eight years a loyal following of people who have consistently appreciated and purchased his work. He sees this rather lonely life style and his singlemindedness as accidental and not self-imposed. Asked about the future, he says in his gentle way that he is quite content with things as they are.

He does, however, talk about possible changes in style, towards a more open and free compositional structure. This is evident in comparing *Untitled, 1971* (ill. p. 152) to *Seeker*, (ill. p. 150), which was painted in 1966.

The current trend towards artistic and intellectual nationalism doesn't interest John Meredith, perhaps because he is a universal rather than a national or international painter; his work is as accessible to a Laplander as to a Vancouverite.

Conversely, however, he feels that national environment has had a part in shaping his work, though he is unable to explain it further than that. He simply believes that he would be a different kind of artist, in some undefined way, if he lived in France rather than in Canada.

John Meredith continues to be one of this country's most intriguing and idiosyncratic young painters; art critics and writers from all over the world are invariably forced to turn in on the work itself, leaving both them and the artist to wonder what it's all about.

John Meredith
Bengal I
oil on canvas
42" x 52"   1962
Dennis Reid Collection,
Ottawa

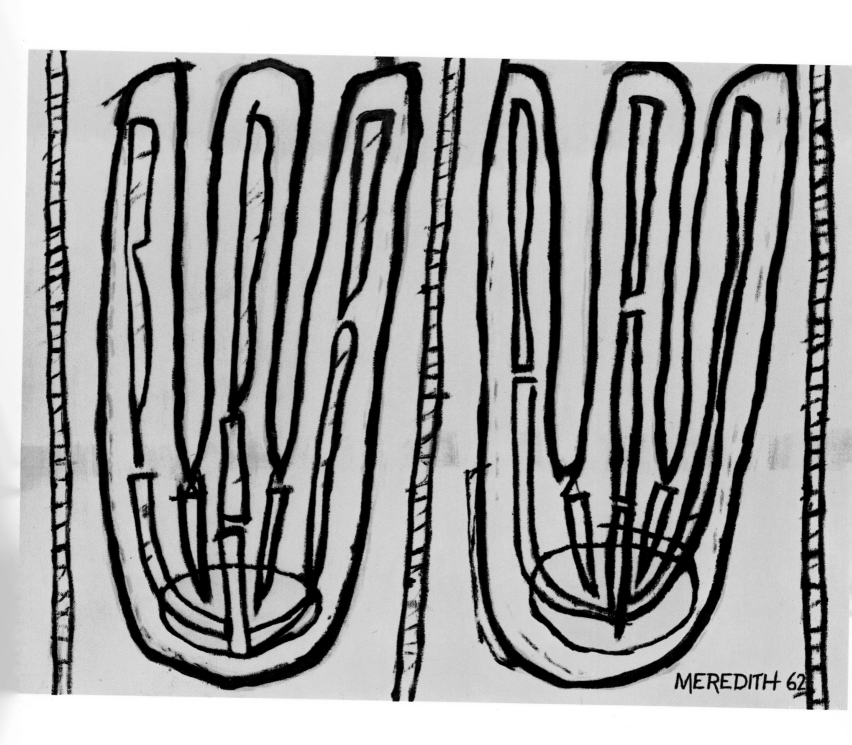

149

John Meredith
Seeker (triptych)
oil on canvas
overall: 70″ x 144¼″,
left & right panels: 70″ x 42″,
centre panel: 70″ x 60¼″
1966
Art Gallery of Ontario,
Toronto

John Meredith
Untitled Diptych, Part I
oil on canvas
96'' x 96''   1968
Jessie & Percy Waxer Collection,
Toronto

John Meredith
Untitled
oil on canvas
60'' x 80''   1971
Mr. & Mrs. Edward Levy,
Toronto

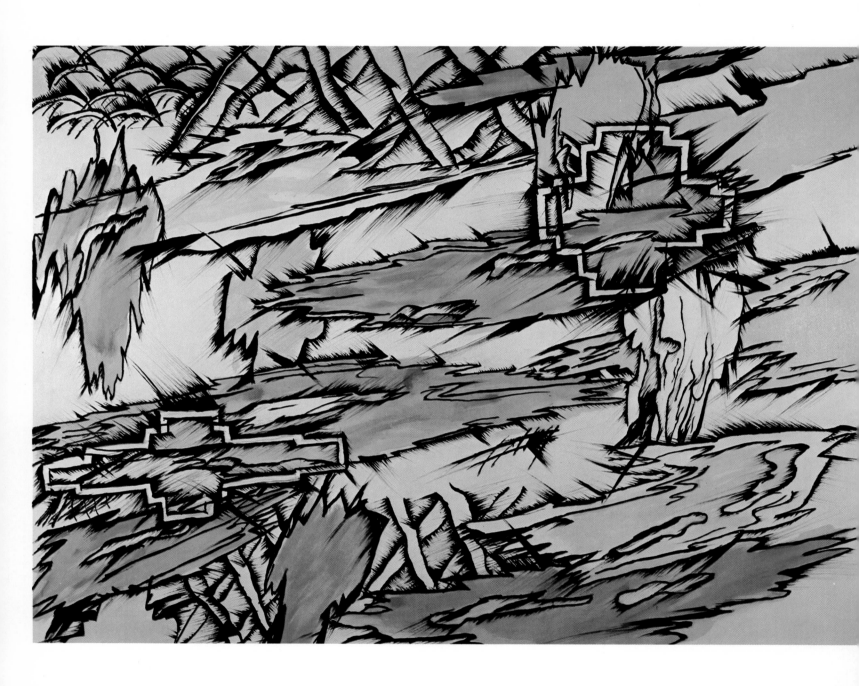

Ted Godwin

I'd rather paint a hundred paintings than write one statement about why. Statements are inevitably painful to write, invariably not really what you wanted to say, and sure to be refuted within six months. Having said that . . . my concern with art seems to be twofold: as a creator and as an artisan.

As a creator every work is the external visual ordering of events concerned with the particular time-continuum I happen to be occupying. Remembered possible conversations and confrontations are spliced tape cuttings of my mind that become the reality of the work. As an artisan the accumulated skills in using tools and materials achieve a formalized ritual that is pleasurable as an end in itself.

Born and raised in Calgary, and trained in painting and sculpture at the Alberta Institute of Technology and Art, Ted Godwin spent the next eight years after graduation, from 1955 to 1963, earning his living in television production and as a designer of neon signs. It is intriguing to note that his paintings from the early sixties are soft and rich, pulsating with a romantic glow. In fact Godwin's *Corners* (ill. p. 157), painted in 1964, shows obvious links with his neon-sign designing experience. And his recent paintings, so much more certain and resolved, still glow with the initial warmth and seductive colour of his first experiments.

But his work in the applied arts was not the only influence upon Godwin. Somehow, leaving his familiar prairie environment became an essential to self-discovery. A Canada Council scholarship enabled him to spend a year in Greece painting full time, and this was a turning point. The same thing seemed to be true of a great many young Canadian painters during the fifties, and to a lesser extent during the sixties, who sought Canada Council money. For a while, the hegira assumed the proportions of a Canadian-art phenomenon — and the disorienting process was apparently as important as the actual freedom from the responsibilities and drudgery of their jobs. In Godwin's case, he came back very much his own man, though with his talent not yet fully matured.

It was at this point that he began attending the Emma Lake Workshops. The first one was in the summer of 1959, the crucial year in which Ronald Bloore (pages 81-8), Roy Kiyooka (pages 89-96) and Arthur McKay brought in the painter Barnett Newman from New York. They had discovered Newman in the black-and-white reproductions accompanying an article in *Art News* and had decided that someone like Newman was needed to counteract the isolation and provincialism of their situations. Along with the rest, Godwin was infected by the experience with even more serious and rigorous ambitions for his work. The next year he returned to attend the seminars under John Ferren; in 1964 he joined the sessions under Jules Olitski and in 1965 those under Lawrence Alloway.

But by this time he had already achieved national recognition as one of the informal group of painters known as "the Regina Five." This was the group of whom the New York critic Clement Greenberg was to write, following his own visit to the Emma Lake Workshops in 1962, "five such fired-up artists would amount to a lot in New York, let alone a city of 125,000." The five consisted of Ronald Bloore (pages 81-8), Kenneth Lochhead (pages 97-104), Arthur McKay, Douglas Morton and Ted Godwin (pages 153-60), and their work as a group had been introduced, in 1961, in a show organized by Bloore himself and called *Five Painters from Regina*. When the show was afterwards reorganized by Richard Simmons, then head of the National Gallery Extension Services, and circulated across Canada, artists and critics in the larger centres were made suddenly aware of the remarkable artistic flowering in Regina.

Godwin was not yet out of his twenties. In an article about his work in the March/April 1962 issue of *Canadian Art,* Richard Simmons called him the least sophisticated of the Regina Five (Greenberg remarked that he was "in transition"), but he was nonetheless doing what Bloore has since described as "bloody good paintings." In the gestural school, they were marked by crowded surfaces, opulent organic forms and his characteristically hedonistic colour. In the same *Canadian Art* article by Simmons, the artist himself was quoted: "My paintings are attempts at exploring, finding and making a cohesive order out of organic accidents that I have willed to take place on canvas. While I have explored organized forms, I find that the naturally evolved forms have more meaning for me. This is achieved by exerting as little control as possible over the initial phase of the painting. . . . Later as I bring my conscious personality to bear, I choose the order most satisfactory to me and elaborate upon it. . . . I do not know what I am painting until it is painted. By this I mean that each change I make dictates another change to be made. The painting only becomes a fact when further elaboration or elimination seems pointless."

It is instructive to compare this with Godwin's very much more recent statement, made in 1972: "My concern with art seems to be twofold: as a creator and as an artisan. As an artisan, the skills in using tools and materials achieve a formalized ritual that is pleasurable as an end in itself. As a creator, every work is the external visual ordering of events concerned with the particular time-continuum I happen to be occupying. Remembered possible conversations and confrontations are spliced tape-cuttings of my mind that become the reality of the work."

The implied suggestion of a new ascendancy of order over chance is indeed apparent in Godwin's recent work. Conditioned as we are to talk about "tough," uncompromising painting, and to take satisfaction in big, authoritative hard-edge composition, it has been easy to criticize his work as being "decorative." But *Brown Trout Tartan Move* 1970 (ill. p. 159), and, indeed, his whole *Tartan* series of the seventies, is perceptibly less romantic and more disciplined than his earlier work — not in its colour but in its geometric, interwoven bands of translucent acrylic paint. The chance aspect of his work has receded, replaced by the presence of the mature controlling mind and spirit, very much in command of his medium.

Big, cheerful and raw-boned, Godwin at thirty-eight looks as though he might be more at home on a ranch than in an artist's studio. But the initial impression is soon belied in conversation by his keen mind and obvious cultural breadth: of particular interest to him is the relationship of music and poetry (he himself writes very well) to the visual arts. Though currently on a sabbatical, in Ireland, he still lives in Regina, where he holds the rank of associate professor at the University of Saskatchewan, Regina Campus, Fine Arts.

Godwin is almost the prototype of the honest western Canadian painter. If, as an isolated provincial, he was first galvanized by the powerful influences from New York that invaded his milieu via the Emma Lake Workshops, he has nonetheless managed to absorb these influences and techniques and make them serve his own special aims. Though he painted with the Regina Five — and shared a studio with Bloore for years — his work shows little similarity to that of the other four. He remains very much his own man.

Ted Godwin
"G" Corners
polymer on canvas
53⅞" x 51"   1964
Art Gallery of Ontario
(Gift from the Georgia J. Weldon Estate
& Canada Council Matching Grant, 1965),
Toronto

Ted Godwin
The Origin of Tartan
elvasite on canvas
36″ x 90″   1967
Collection of the artist

Ted Godwin
Brown Trout Tartan Move
elvasite & oil on canvas
79″ x 113″   1970
Collection of the artist

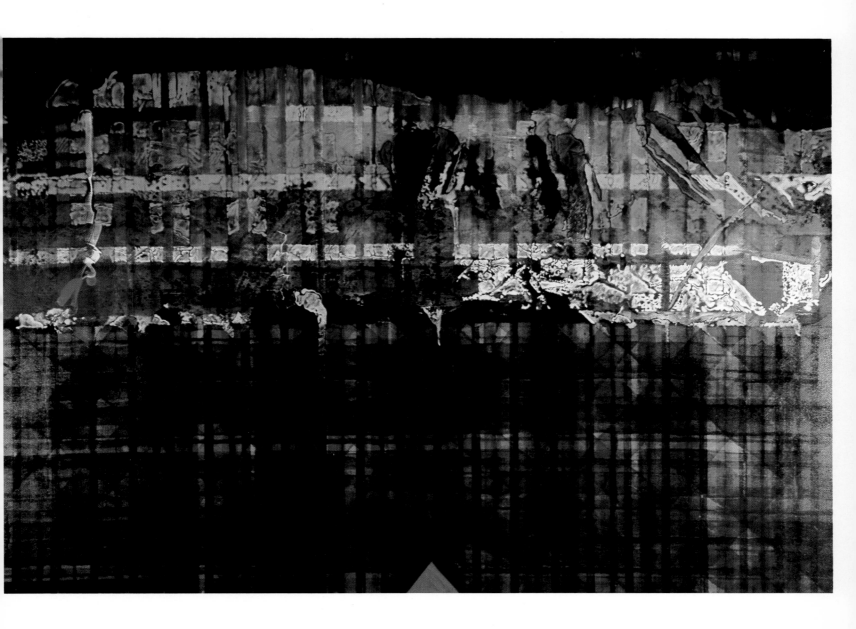

Ted Godwin
The Orange Popsicle Tartan
elvasite & oil on canvas
114″ x 114″ 1970
Collection of the artist

Guido Molinari

Ma préoccupation structurelle fondamentale pose que la série n'est pas constituée par des objets plus ou moins analogiques, que de fait les quantitiés analogiques, si elles existent dans la matérialité du tableau, ne peuvent exister dans la perception. Par là, le tableau échappe radicalement à la notion de la notion de quantité pour se fonder à celle de qualité, c'est-à-dire sur l'elaboration d'un système qui permettre de multiples autres fonctions. C'est par là seulement que peut s'établir une véritable hiérarchie signifiante fondée sur le pleine réalité des variables des éléments.

Il n'existe pas en effet dans la perception d'objets identiques et c'est dans la perception de l'equivoque, de la naissance des multiplicités qu'est donnée au spectateur la possibilité de s'impliquer dans la fonction sémantique du tableau.

Cette façon de concevoir la série, à l'opposé de celle de la majorité des artistes qui ont pensé l'utiliser, repose sur la notion d'individuation, d'hétérogénéité foncière de la chafne des éléments d'une même couleur. C'est en posant la capacité de la couleur à opérer un nombre indéfini de permutations que se constitue, à mes yeux, le ressort dynamique créateur des espaces fictifs qui engendre l'expérience de la spatialité; excluant par définition la notion d'un espace spécifique donné. Ce n'est qu'à partir de la notion du devenir impliqué dans l'acte de perception que la structure s'expérimente et se fonde comme expérience existentielle.

Guido Molinari is a giant figure on the landscape of Canadian art, as a painter and as the acknowledged leader and spokesman for French-Canadian artists, both in Quebec and throughout the country.

David Thompson, highly respected art critic of the London *Times*, writing in the catalogue for the Canada Council Collection, circulated by the National Gallery of Canada in 1969, said of Molinari's work: "[it] is colour painting that works, not on the nerves, but on the emotions, and a manipulation of colour contrast in which tension and brilliance are remarkably allied to spaciousness and – a quality that only one or two Canadian painters can match – a solid, unhurried grandeur of presence."

There is nothing tentative or indecisive about Molinari's work; for some years now he has produced paintings of mature power and clarity of vision. His *Mutation*, for example (ill. p. 167), is reminiscent of a musical chord, vibrating rich colours in complex juxtaposition with each other. David Thompson, speaking of Molinari's colours generally, says, "The effect is less of the energy of colour than of its resonance and orchestration." Molinari's work is genuinely a triumph of the whole over the parts: the latter are cunningly simple, but have been put together to form a whole of massive integrity and beauty.

The musical references which Molinari calls forth are appropriate: he was born of Italian parentage in Montreal, where his father was a musician. His maternal grandfather had a studio casting figures in plaster, rather like the inexpensive and popular art of that time. Molinari was at ease in the artistic atmosphere and decided early to become an artist.

In 1948, the year of Borduas' tradition-shattering *Refus Global*, Molinari, then fifteen and still in high school, enrolled at L'Ecole des Beaux Arts for night classes. At that time these classes were extremely academic and Molinari found them inhibiting, a precocious, but accurate, judgement. Molinari was fortunate: the comings and goings in the family home included artists – students of Borduas and followers of Les Automatistes, among others – and he had become interested in them while still a child. Before he was in his teens, he remembers, he talked to these men and studied their paintings; he also recalls seeing the first Automatiste exhibit in 1949, an event which made him conscious of the international non-figurative movement.

Like Tousignant, Molinari studied at the art school of the Montreal Museum of Fine Art, where one of his teachers was Gordon Webber. By the time he was seventeen, Molinari had committed himself to personal research and was curious about the Automatiste belief that painting could be done automatically, intuitively, out of the subconscious. Molinari blindfolded himself and painted in the dark in order to explore fully the concept of spontaneous, gestural painting about which Borduas and his circle talked. In spite of Molinari's conclusion, which rejected the claims of the Automatistes, he produced six important paintings in that style. In the eight month period of experimentation, Molinari also tried the drip technique of Jackson Pollock and the pallet knife application of paint favoured by Borduas. *Emergence* (ill. p. 165) is an example of the latter.

The history of art is littered with the battles of two basically opposed forces, both of which have contributed richly to our visual experience: those for whom painting is an expression of the intuitive, the emotional, the poetic, and those for whom it is cerebral — formal, disciplined, carefully thought out. In the early fifties, that battle was being waged fiercely in Montreal and Molinari was a vigorous participant. Far from wanting to follow what was going on in New York, Borduas and his disciples, adherents of the emotional side of the argument, were antagonistic to it; they found Pollock too mechanical, not poetic enough. Up to the middle of the 1950s Borduas was held in such personal reverence that the concept of automatisme had not been fully aired in the art world. But a show, *Materière Chant*, at the Montreal Museum of Fine Art ended that era; one of the judges of the show, which was the last flowering of automatisme, was Borduas, who had been invited back from New York for the event. Molinari took his stand by refusing to exhibit in the show — a particularly bold action from a young artist, but inevitable for a man who had decided that he had to take a stand in opposition to the automatistes.

From the decline of one artistic idea another, inevitably, rose: in the same year, 1954, came a reaction from a group who called themselves Les Plasticiens and whose works were cool, hard-edged, geometric abstractions. Although not ever a formal member of Les Plasticiens, Molinari found in its output a concept close to his own; in time, after the group had disbanded, Molinari became the acknowledged leader of Plasticien-type painters.

Molinari was then pursuing a type of painting we now call hard-edge. He claims that his inspiration for this came from watching garages paint automobile bodies using masking tape. He also says that this innovation preceded any knowledge of the hard-edge style from New York; e.g., Ellsworth Kelly, who was at that time still in France. In retrospect it appears that the Borduas circle in Montreal and Painters Eleven in Toronto were engaged in "action painting" of a type which became known by its New York practitioners as abstract expressionism, while Molinari and his loosely formed group were well into hard-edge.

Like Tousignant, Molinari had found that there were only two galleries where he could hope to exhibit and one of these was attached to a restaurant. Molinari (with Tousignant and Robert Blair) founded the Galerie l'Actuelle;

at considerable cost to the time he should be devoting to his own work, Molinari acted as director. He says of this period: "We were the atheists of painting," meaning that they were striving for an art based on its own formal values and divorced from spiritual or emotional associations.

Out of the gallery experience, and the contacts it provided with other young artists, Molinari moved firmly into position as a leader of the painting community; for a period, in fact, he was engaged more as an artistic polemicist than as an artist. He is physically suited for the role: though short and slight, he has a mobile body and a strong expressive face with a suitably prominent Roman nose. Sometimes his skin seems alabaster pale and old, at other times he looks surprisingly youthful; what is most impressive however is the sense of presence, of dignity and integrity that he radiates. He expresses himself fluently and pointedly in either French or English and discusses ideas with the greatest of ease in either tongue. Molinari is all of a piece: it is hard to imagine that a man who speaks as he does could paint in any way other than the one he uses.

The man's self control is evident in a consistency of mood — he is articulate and precise whether teaching painting at Sir George Williams University in downtown Montreal or working in his studio in a converted boxing gymnasium in Montreal's gritty north end. In the studio, under brilliant electric lamps, he darts about like some reincarnation of the boxers who once trained there, efficiently pulling from the giant racks which line the dark perimeters of the gym, dozens and dozens of his immense canvases.

Molinari has meticulously catalogued and photographed his output, for he is confident of his place in art history — at the forefront. His estimate doesn't seem unrealistic: no serious show of modern Canadian art, either at home or abroad, had been mounted since 1965 that did not include at least one example of Molinari's work. Among the major foreign exhibits in which he has been represented are the Museum of Modern Art's *The Responsive Eye* (1965), The Guggenheim Fourth International Awards Exhibition held in New York (1964) and the crowning goal of any artist's ambitions, the Venice Biennale (1968).

Molinari doesn't lend himself to artistic comparison shopping; confronting one of his paintings, the viewer isn't tempted to stack Molinari up against someone else. The paintings simply exist to be experienced by the viewer; one reacts to them, in the mountain-climbing cliché, "because they are there."

Guido Molinari
Emergence
oil on canvas
26″ x 21″   1955
Collection of the artist

Guido Molinari
Equivalence
acrylic on canvas
49'' x 58''   1959
Collection of the artist

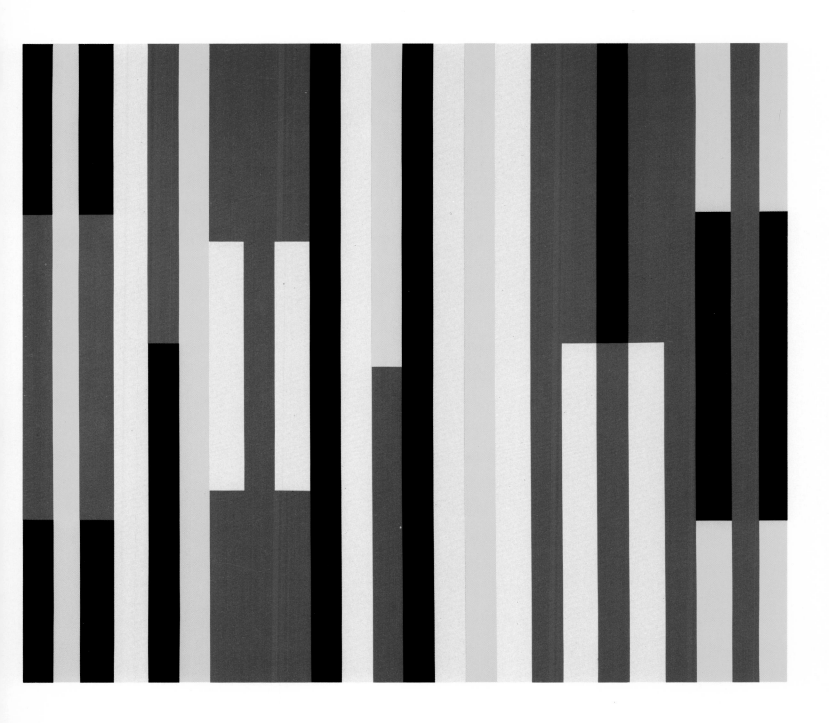

Guido Molinari
Mutation Sérielle Verte-Rouge
acrylic on canvas
81'' x 98''   1966
Art Gallery of Ontario
(Purchase, Corporations'
Subscription Endowment, 1967),
Toronto

Guido Molinari
Structure Triangulaire Rose-Orange
acrylic on canvas
68'' x 68''   1971
Collection of the artist

Yves Gaucher

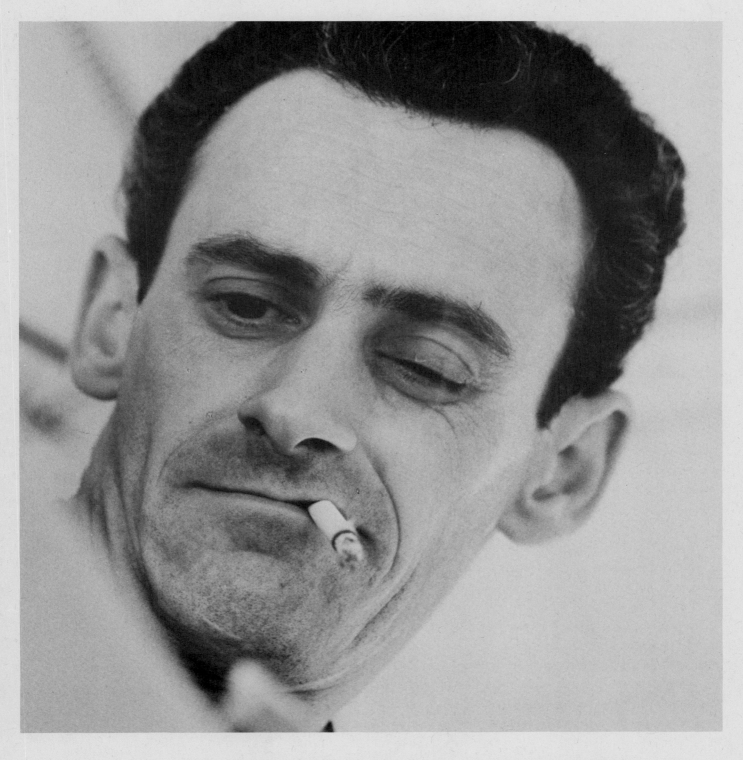

We don't really change, we just become ourselves, but more so all the time.

Unlike the South American or European traditions, where the arts have been treated harmoniously, North American artists have tended to segregate themselves — the painters from the musicians, the musicians from the poets, the poets from the architects. This splintering has been perhaps more noticeable in English than in French Canada, where, for instance, Borduas' circle included poets and writers. When and if there is a cross-pollination in Canadian arts, either French or English, it has been not because of but rather in spite of the formal art education system.

Yves Gaucher of Montreal was singularly fortunate in being born into a musical home and this fact has had the greatest influence on his art. He was the sixth in a family of eight, son of a druggist and optician, his mother a serious musician who played piano and sang. Gaucher remembers that the family, in which every member played an instrument, was somewhat competitive; his first music lessons were given by his mother and he recalls this as the most significant experience of his childhood.

As a result, Gaucher sees no dichotomy in art: the aesthetic experience is a unity stemming from an appreciation of the same basic principles that underlie any art form, whether auditory or visual. Aesthetic experience is, in Gaucher's works, something he can now "live by rather than live up to," which was the case when he was a child.

From the time Gaucher was five years of age he was educated at boarding schools, where insubordination led to his expulsion from a series of institutions. When he was twelve, he obtained permission to study music at the school he was attending; he could have chosen any instrument, but, for some reason he no longer remembers, the trumpet was the only one he could practise on for as long as he wanted, up to four hours a day, in order to become a member of the school symphony orchestra. So he picked it.

Gaucher took his trumpet home during the holidays and practised all day, in order to become a soloist; even his musician mother seemed to find his perseverance difficult to endure: when he was again expelled and came home to work for his father, she refused to allow him to buy a trumpet with his earnings.

In his early teens, Gaucher became interested in the visual arts: he had seen the Greek drawings that illustrated a text used in his classical studies — and, he says, was once expelled for making drawings of a bare-breasted sphinx he had copied out of an encyclopedia; that may be an over-simplification, but his explanation in those terms says something of his rebellious nature.

When Gaucher was seventeen, he had become so interested in his music, especially in serious jazz, that he gave up his academic studies completely. From then until he was twenty, he played in various bands at night, holding down an office job with Imperial Oil during the day; but he became increasingly frustrated by his lack of formal musical schooling and felt that he was reaching for a level of musicianship beyond what he had been trained for, up to that point.

In that same period he was also becoming more involved in art: he had begun to draw and paint in water colours; he was concerned enough about his work to seek the advice of Arthur Lismer, Group of Seven artist and at that time a leading teacher in Montreal. Gaucher remembers his reception from Lismer as cool; Lismer told him that if he were serious about his art, he would have to quit his job and study full time. Gaucher left Imperial Oil and enrolled at L'Ecole des Beaux Arts, a comparatively late starter at twenty.

The year was 1954; Borduas had returned from New York to judge the La Materière Chant exhibition and the Montreal art colony was in the midst of a noisy controversy over him and Les Automatistes. L'Actuelle, the new commercial gallery, Guido Molinari and Claude Tousignant (pages 161-8 and 137-44) were showing their work; Gaucher arranged a couple of jazz programs for L'Actuelle. He recalls that he wasn't impressed with the work he saw there, because he wasn't then thinking seriously about that kind of Mondrian-inspired art. The scene was exciting for a young artist and Gaucher still remembers it vividly.

The next year, following what had become a pattern for him, Gaucher was expelled from L'Ecole des Beaux Arts for insubordination — his unwillingness to follow the prescribed course of studies. Looking back, he feels that his departure from the school was beneficial and he thenceforth pursued his education on his own. At the time Gaucher was keeping himself by working at odd jobs, including a stint as a Fuller Brush salesman.

In 1959, after a lengthy period of artistic exploration and self-teaching, Gaucher felt ready to buy his own press; he was becoming known for his organic, somewhat romantic prints, reminiscent of the forms used by Les Automatistes. In a short period he achieved an astonishing pre-eminence and became Canada's leading experimental printmaker.

His forms were developing, becoming more disciplined, denser and geometric, in growing harmony with his interest in music. All during the fifties he had studied recordings of Indian ragas and the music of Stockhausen, Anton Webern and Luigi Nono; in 1961 he attended a concert of Webern music in Paris, an event which had a profound effect on Gaucher and which determined his next stage of development.

He returned to Montreal to continue his study of Webern's music and to translate his understanding of it into visual forms. In 1963 he produced a series of prints titled *En Hommage à Webern*, and that composer's music continues to exert an influence on his work to the present day.

In the mid-sixties, Gaucher moved seriously into painting with a series of square canvases designed to hang on the diagonal (*Circular Motion*, ill. p. 174). Forms and lines in his Webern paintings and prints pulsate against vivid colour and he was classified, at the time, as an op artist, though his disciplined crafts-manship and almost scientific experimentation with optical laws make many more demands on the viewer.

Gradually, Gaucher moved away from the bright op colours and easy visual illusions to undertake a more difficult task — to pin to his canvases silence, as well as sound, paralleling Webern's music, which is concerned with these pauses. In 1968 he produced another set of prints, called *Transitions*, based on Webern's work; these led directly to his large grey paintings, with their flat expanses and their fine, white lines emerging only after minutes of optical and cerebral concentration. This need to focus one's complete attention gives his work a dimension of time which is more readily found in music than in most painting, a singular fulfilment of Gaucher's aim. With an understanding of Gaucher's unique success in bringing together the musical and the visual, the viewer is enabled to appreciate the richness behind the austere surfaces of his work.

Like a composer following every possible artistic avenue opened by his choice musical form — in the fugue, for example — Gaucher explores his chosen form to the fullest, in a series of paintings and prints. *Cardinal Raga*, 1967 (ill. p. 175), is one of a group based on the raga. In the grey series there are now almost a hundred prints and paintings of various sizes, ranging from a foot or two square to one that is nine by fifteen feet.

Yves Gaucher is a tall, spare man, thoughtful and intense, his angular frame in harmony with his disciplined work. Though he lives comfortably in a middle class section of Montreal, supporting his young family from his work and his teaching, he sees the role of the artist in society in uncompromisingly indivi-dualistic terms. The place of the artist, he says, is really in the "underground": free of any political or social system, resistant to any attempt at regimentation or marching in lockstep. On the contrary, the artist must remain "out of step" because he is a free thinker, not for sale either to government or to the rest of society. "The artist," he states, "is the guy who keeps everyone and everything awake."

He believes that any human being, working in his studio *alone*, doing what *he* has to do in order to keep his own artistic integrity, is, in a sense, subversive, running counter to the current mode. Gaucher's contribution is that, working in this self-imposed isolation, he is able to produce works of spare beauty to enrich his fellows.

Yves Gaucher
Le Cercle de Grande Réserve
acrylic on canvas
60'' x 60''   1965
Art Gallery of Ontario
(Gift from the McLean Foundation, 1966),
Toronto

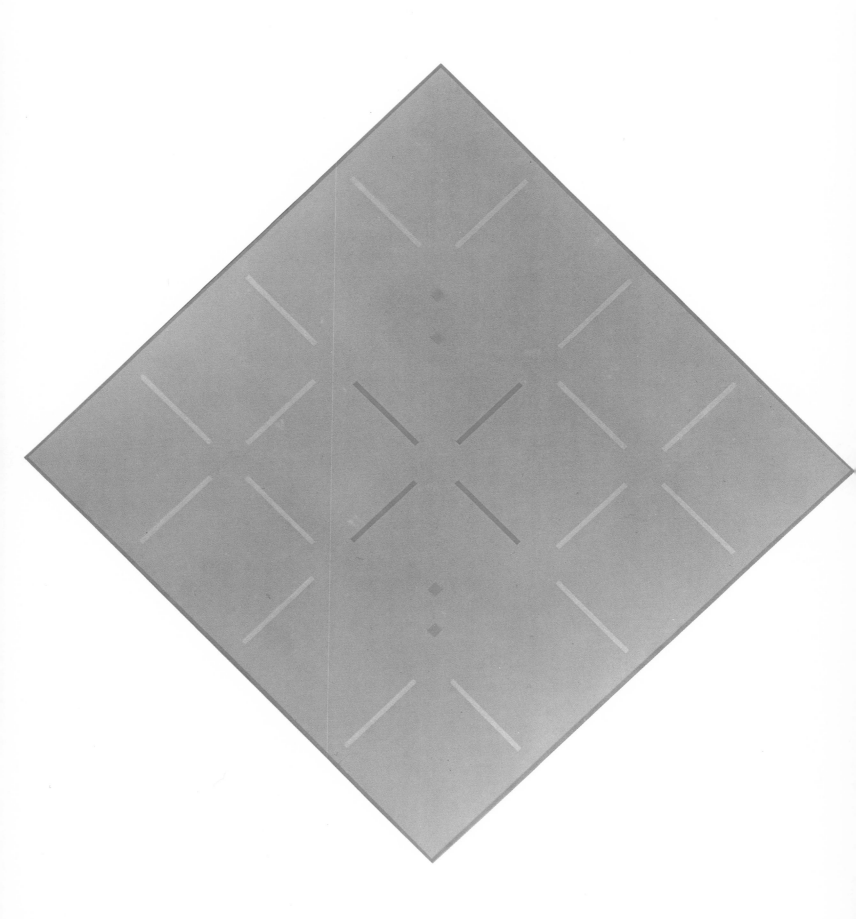

Yves Gaucher
Circular Motion
acrylic on canvas
84'' x 84''   1965
York University,
Toronto

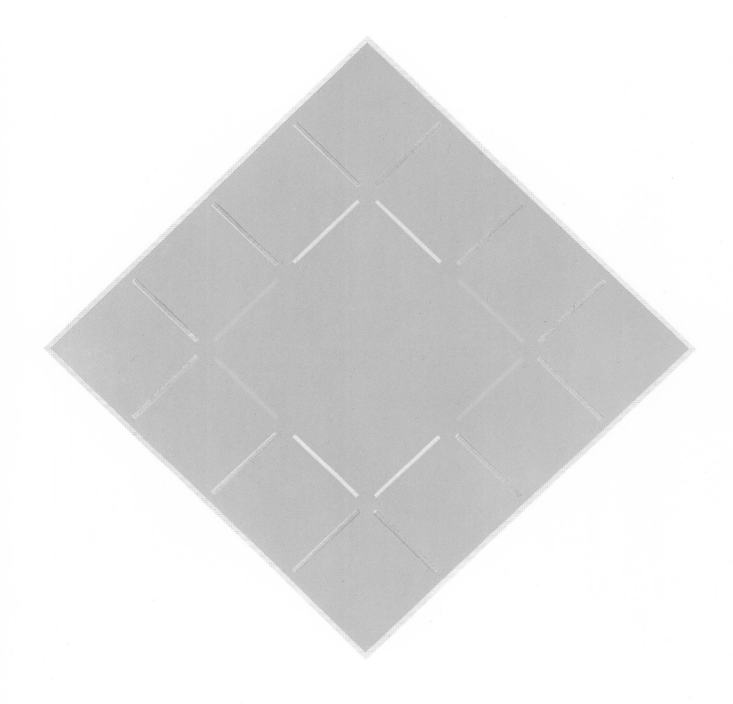

Yves Gaucher
Cardinal Raga
acrylic on canvas
72″ x 72″   1967
York University,
Toronto

Yves Gaucher
Bleu, Vert, Bleu
acrylic on canvas
80'' x 92''   1971
Marlborough/Godard Gallery,
Toronto

Gordon Rayner

My statement has to do, in a way, with 24 hours a day all the time.

I prefer a reality as close to my dreams as possible; consequently what I have to do outside of my dreams is to make more of my time the way I would like it ideally. Part of the struggle is just the pain and pleasure of creating art.

The kind of art I want to create is my own kind ... nobody else's. I paint paintings I want to look at ... I make music I want to hear.

If it is against the grain or if it is unpopular that is too bad ... just too bad.

The concept of the "past as prologue" is one generally revered by art historians: it is pleasing to be able to follow the work of an artist, to see his first, derivative student efforts give way to more mature paintings that have the stamp of an individual personality on them. Sometimes it is possible, seeing an artist's oeuvre laid out, as in a catalogue, to trace the development almost as if it were a slow motion film being unwound. The process is a comfortable one for the critic and collector, making it easy to assess a given work in the context of the whole and to await eagerly the next inevitable and (always in retrospect) prefigured step.

Gordon Rayner is cold comfort for those who like the step-by-step art game: he never allows past work to define his style. Just when the art *cognoscenti* think they've got him pegged as a romantic, abstract northern landscapist (see *Magnetawan,* 1965, ill. p. 182) he turns to glowing and intricate geometric forms (*Love in the Jungle,* 1969, ill. p. 183). Then, just as the unwary are sighing with relief and saying, "Ah, *that's* what Rayner's about," he produces a mural, for the outside wall of a downtown Toronto office building, which depicts a Canadian forest in cool, precise terms.

Barrie Hale, writing in *artscanada* (February 1970) of Rayner's seven one-man shows in the sixties said, "Certainly, within each there was such a variety of pictorial attack, such a range of method and means (and indeed within any given work, such a range of method and means), it almost appeared that in the obviously large intelligence at work, there was a perverse one, bent, in its rough way, towards earnest anarchy." The artist himself put it succinctly in the epigraph for one of those exhibits: "Each work [is] single, alone, 'disinterested' and irrelevant to all proceeding works."

The most rewarding thing about Rayner's art is that he has an abundant talent that keeps him from getting lost in the byways of all that he attempts. His approach doesn't reflect a paucity of inspiration, but rather a restless curiosity combined with an appropriate appreciation of his own powers.

Rayner's eclecticism has its roots in his experiences as a very young man and his biography is instructive for those who seek to understand the sources of his talent; it may also provide some partial answer to those who wonder "what makes an artist?"

Gordon Rayner was born in Toronto in 1935, son and nephew of successful commercial artists, grandson of an English landscape painter and great-grandson of a member of the Royal Academy. Father and son were close and, because the elder Rayner had left school to pursue a career, the younger one decided to choose that course, trusting that his father would provide an entrée into the world of commercial art. Instead, his father insisted he try making his own way and, giving him the yellow pages from the telephone book, told him (according to Rayner), "Start at A under the commercial artist section and keep walking."

The young man did – without success – until he reached the ws, where he was hired as an apprentice in the firm of w-b-w. Perhaps the moral for students of the what-makes-an-artist school is that it takes at least some blind luck: the b in the firm name was Jack Bush (pages 49-56). Rayner was apprenticed to Bush and remembers "washing coffee cups and looking over Jack's shoulder for two years"; his pay was eighteen dollars weekly.

Other than this apprenticing experience, which had a considerable effect on him, Rayner has never had any formal art training: art at high school didn't really mean much – he took it only because he found it an easy subject.

Jack Bush was to have a continuing influence on Rayner: as one of the Painters Eleven it was he who introduced the young man to the group as it was being formed in 1953. Rayner acted as messenger boy for the artists and re-members the all-night meetings, the arguments and the fights about art when feelings were so fierce that Oscar Cahen and Harold Town (pages 73-80) some-times thrashed about the floor. Despite his role as mascot and privileged insider, Rayner remained largely unimpressed with "fine art" and determined to make his own career in the field of commercial design.

Long after Rayner left the commercial studio, Jack Bush continued to be helpful, though Rayner refused to follow his example and attend the night school life classes which Bush faithfully took in order to improve his drawing skills – even after he left figurative art for abstract. Rayner was singularly unaffected by Bush's later dramatic change to colour-field painting and re-members that he thought at the time that it was "peculiar."

In the same period, however, Rayner saw two films, *Lust for Life* and *Moulin Rouge,* and their seductive presentation of la vie bohémienne made him decide that the painter's life was for him: an anecdote which will fit in well if Rayner's life story is every made into a movie. He was still less interested in the hard work of painting pictures than in the supposed life of wine, women, song and the casual creation of masterpieces.

At about that time, Rayner left w-b-w to take the first of twelve trips to Europe; he stayed for two years, returning to various jobs – from junior positions to art directing – in commercial houses. Though the trips, interspersed with commercial work, became a pattern that lasted for about six years, Rayner had a goal in mind: he would become a serious artist by the time he was thirty. He had begun going on northern sketching trips with his father, much in the Group of Seven manner, but was painting in a more naturalistic style than that the Group had used. His paintings, along with those of Joyce Wieland, made up the first exhibit in Avrom Isaacs' tiny new Greenwich Gallery in Toronto.

Rayner was a precocious young artist, but his style was that of the nineteenth-century realists; his next breakthrough as a painter had its genesis in, of all places, a smart-alecky article on Jackson Pollock in *Life*. The accompanying photographs of Pollock's work galvanized Rayner — he was enraged by what he saw, correctly, as the end of the kind of work he was doing and thought was the "end of art" itself. "I was moved as I have never been since about anything," he recalls. "I wanted to march in protest against this movement." Instead, his intense concern motivated him to make several trips to New York where, with great concentration, he went from gallery to gallery, studying the paintings in them. There he first saw the work of de Kooning, the giant of the New York school of abstract expressionism — in Rayner's estimation "the greatest single influence on the young painters of my generation" and still an art hero of his. His style showed the effects of the artistic shaking-up he was going through and, in his own words, he "graduated from doing second-rate impressionism to doing second-rate abstract expressionism."

But Rayner's conversion was not enthusiastically greeted in all of Toronto's art circles: like most of the young artists of the Isaacs group, vulnerable to the artistic bombardment from New York in the fifties, he was regularly rejected from professional art society shows, although a piece of his welded sculpture was accepted by the Ontario Society of the Artists for an annual exhibition.

In 1964, a year before his self-imposed limit for entering the "serious" art world had been reached, Rayner left commercial art to become a full-time painter and sold enough of his works to survive. During the late sixties he received a number of Canada Council grants; he was instrumental in persuading the Council to make a major change in its policy. Rayner and others felt that the Council's philosophy of restricting awards to study abroad was absurd at a time when many young artists were in need of support for the exciting artistic ventures that interested them; he took part in a protest march on the Council, and it subsequently made grants to cover the costs of film, the purchase of materials, and living expenses incurred when artists planned to work at home. Rayner himself was the first recipient of such an award, used for a film he was making.

Rayner is a big, burly, but soft-spoken man; heavily moustached, he must look very at home in the north woods he loves and so often uses as a source of his art. He now earns his living painting and teaching at the New School in Toronto. He feels that teaching keeps him on his toes and isn't as dangerous for the serious artist as commercial art which, he says, "seduces with its tricky clichés, impossible to keep out of your fine art. They get under your fingers and subconsciously get in the way of finding solutions for fine art problems."

There is no way of divining what Gordon Rayner's art will be like in the future, though his talent ensures that it will be worth following. One thing is almost certain — it won't be like his work of the past.

Gordon Rayner
Aquarium
oil on canvas
60'' x 48''   1962
The Isaacs Gallery Collection,
Toronto

Gordon Rayner
Magnetawan
acrylic on canvas
70" x 60"   1965
D. Perlmutter Collection,
Toronto

Gordon Rayner
Love in the Jungle
acrylic on canvas
84'' x 116''   1969
The Isaacs Gallery Collection,
Toronto

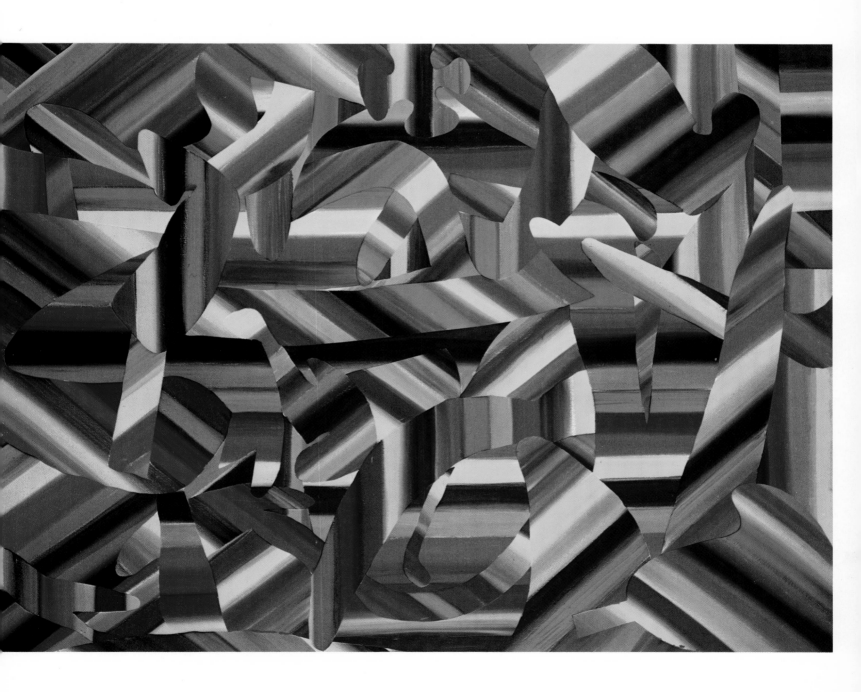

Gordon Rayner
Wall Mural
acrylic & latex
73' x 110'   1971
Location: York & Front Sts., Toronto;
one of a series of Art Walls
commissioned by Benson & Hedges
Tobacco Company for cities across Canada

Greg Curnoe

I make no distinction between art and life so that what I have said applies equally to my art or whatever else I do.

Art in Canada is seldom approached in a light-hearted manner, particularly by artists, who tend to think and talk about it in terms that sometimes approach the quasi-religious. In true style, Greg Curnoe, most Dadaist of our painters, has taken a huge delight in bringing off the startling and unexpected, whether shocking viewers with obscenities stamped on his canvases or discomfiting the Canadian government in executing a commission for it.

Nonetheless, in 1969, Greg Curnoe was chosen by the National Gallery to represent Canada at the Tenth Biennial of contemporary international art in Sao Paulo; Dennis Reid, who wrote the text of the accompanying catalogue, said, "Curnoe seems to be faced with the paradox that for something to be accepted as a serious statement, it must first be accepted as Art, and that, once it has been accepted as Art, it immediately becomes something which is removed from any direct relevance to life. For many people, the recognition of an art object seems to preclude any further involvement with that thing. Curnoe has tried to sidestep the whole issue by making pictures which may not be identified as art until it is too late; until their direct statements have made some impact." Curnoe himself has said, "I'm afraid of art because it might kill me." His determination to pierce the bored reverence with which many people approach art is one factor in making him an important artist in Canada.

Curnoe is always pushing ideas to the limit. He writes poetry, makes films, is a prime mover in an artists' "union," the Canadian Artists' Representation.

Greg Curnoe's work doesn't lend itself easily to explanation or criticism, dealing as it does with activities which operate outside the normal and traditional boundaries of "art." John Chandler, writing in the April 1969 *artscanada,* says, ". . . we are so conditioned to seeing art as that which is exhibited, that we have lost sight of the fact that art is also a process, an activity whose products are merely evidence that art has taken or is taking place. . . . It is still perhaps necessary to judge the gardening by the garden, the activity by the accomplishment, but we must guard against the assumption that the accomplishment is the cause of the activity; there may indeed be more to it than meets the eye. Such, I think, is the case with Greg Curnoe, who asks the spectator if he is reading him or just looking."

Reading, of course, is an operative word in discussing Curnoe: his trademark is his use of stamped words, not only in his pictures but as complete pictures themselves. The panels from *True North Strong and Free* (ill. p. 190) are fairly typical of the lettering paintings which are word pictures — an aspect of pop art that Curnoe very early earmarked for himself. Letterism is not new in painting: words have been used to supplement or in some cases to form pictures at several points in art history. Cubism, for example, first drew the present century's attention to the idea; in the fifties it was in vogue in Europe and in the sixties in the u.s. Curnoe's work in this idiom sometimes looks like that of the American painter Shusaku Arawaka but is much less formal and thus has a different effect on the viewer.

Using the international pop style filtered through his Dada attitude, Curnoe, nonetheless, resolutely concentrates on his immediate environment as the source of his subject matter: his home town of London, Ontario.

There he was born and educated in a middle class family whose lifestyle gives no clues to the path he has chosen to pursue.

A graduate of the justly praised art course at Beal Tech, he attended the Doon School of Art near Kitchener, Ontario, and, finally, the Ontario College of Art in Toronto, where he graduated in 1960.

He became interested in Dada, joining the Société pour l'Etude du Mouvement Dada, partly through the influence of Professor Michael Sanouillet of the University of Toronto, who was international president of the society. In the late fifties, artists in New York, using the concept that art is not necessarily a product, but is a process, staged the first "happening," a specific event they labelled as art. Not surprisingly, considering his views, Curnoe initiated the first Canadian happening, which he titled "Celebration," in London in 1962.

A little earlier, Curnoe and some of his friends had begun to publish a magazine, *Region*, for which he wrote; he has also been published in James Reaney's *Alphabet* magazine and in the more recent *20 Cents*, another regional publication of art criticism and review, now defunct.

Curnoe's writing is, if anything, even more specifically anti-American than his paintings: in very un-English-Canadian style he has been involved in the proclamation of several manifestoes, the most recent being an anti-American statement he co-authored with artist John Boyle. He calls it *Refus Continental*, because of its strongly-worded repudiation of the continentalism of many Canadians.

Whatever one's political views, Curnoe must be admired for his remarkably consistent stance: in 1968, invited to do a cover for the domestic edition of *Time*, he refused. Two years later, asked this time to do a cover for the international edition, he again said no on a matter of anti-American principle.

In 1968, Curnoe's views, as expressed in one of his works, embroiled him in a quarrel with the Department of Transport. As part of its continuing program of placing art in Canada's airports, the Department had commissioned the artist to do a 500-foot-long mural for the international section of Montreal's Dorval airport; the theme, according to the officials at Transport, was to be airship travel. They were not amused on first viewing the work (Curnoe had put it into place without consulting them) to find that it included among other things, a bloodied figure, lying on its back, which bore a striking resemblance to U.S. President Lyndon Johnson; a reference to Muhammed Ali, then out of favour in the States; as well as a scene of airship bombings. "What we wanted," one official said wistfully, "was something nice, gay and colourful." Curnoe maintained that he had no intention of embarrassing the government, but the offending panels were removed and have never been replaced.

In the same year, Curnoe became involved in another contretemps, this one at the Edinburgh Festival show, *Canada 101*: a series of stamped lettrist paintings, *Twenty-Four Hourly Notes* (1966), describing the artist's activities over a twenty-four hour period (one panel for each hour), was removed from the exhibition because of "allegedly obscene passages."

Greg Curnoe, probably best-known of the London School (partly because of his cross-country speaking engagements on behalf of the Canadian Artists' Representation and in defence of anti-Americanism), resists nonetheless the idea that he is a leader of that group. He doesn't teach, insists that there are no "stars," only "members of a community" who support and stimulate each other. His family and friends are important to his pre-occupation with "sense of place." In his view of *Victoria Hospital* (ill. p. 192), Curnoe numbers certain objects and provides a key to them; many of these numbers refer to specific places, i.e., number written is another example of the importance with which he invests location.

Curnoe's paintings show change, but it is in terms of variety, rather than being an evolution of style. The works illustrated range over a period of seven years, though anyone but an ardent Curnoe-watcher might be excused for thinking all had been produced in any one of those years.

Greg Curnoe always presents himself as a regional artist but his paintings are, if anything, evidence that abstract art defies regionalism. Where the painting is close to realism (as in *Victoria Hospital*) it may be possible for the person who knows London, Ontario, to place the scene. But much of Curnoe's work is regional only because he says it is and says so *on the paintings*, by using lettrism.

Pop art imagery uses the objects of the everyday world as its subject; at its best is "written" in trenchant prose. Curnoe is a pop artist in his use of pop art images, stylistic devices and colours to "say" what is on his mind. Pop art is an ideal style for an aggressive message like anti-Americanism: it uses the grotesque and even touches burlesque on occasion to maintain a cool, objective stance but, to make his message focused and unambiguous, Curnoe needs words.

It is ironic that Canada's two most nationalistic artists, Curnoe and Wieland (pages 121-8), should, at the same time, be our leading practitioners of an art style invented in England and brought to full fruition in the United States.

Greg Curnoe
Spring on the Ridgeway
oil on plywood, rayon/nylon,
metal, wood, paper, string
overall: 73⁵/₈″ x 73⁵/₈″,
left panel: 36¹/₄″ x 27¹³/₁₆″
1964
Art Gallery of Ontario,
Toronto

Greg Curnoe
The True North Strong and Free, Nos. 1-5
No. 1, polyurethane & marking ink on paper on plywood;
Nos. 2-5, polyurethane & ink on plywood
23¹/₂'' x 25'' each   1968
London Public Library &
Art Museum Collection,
London, Ontario

Greg Curnoe
Heart of London
acrylic, plastic & marking ink on
plywood, with electric lights attached
diameter: 110''   1967
National Gallery of Canada,
Ottawa

Greg Curnoe
View of Victoria Hospital, 3rd series
oil, wallpaper & marking ink on plywood,
with stereo speakers attached,
cassette player tape recording &
printed legend included
96'' x 191³/₄''   1969-71
National Gallery of Canada,
Ottawa

Claude Breeze

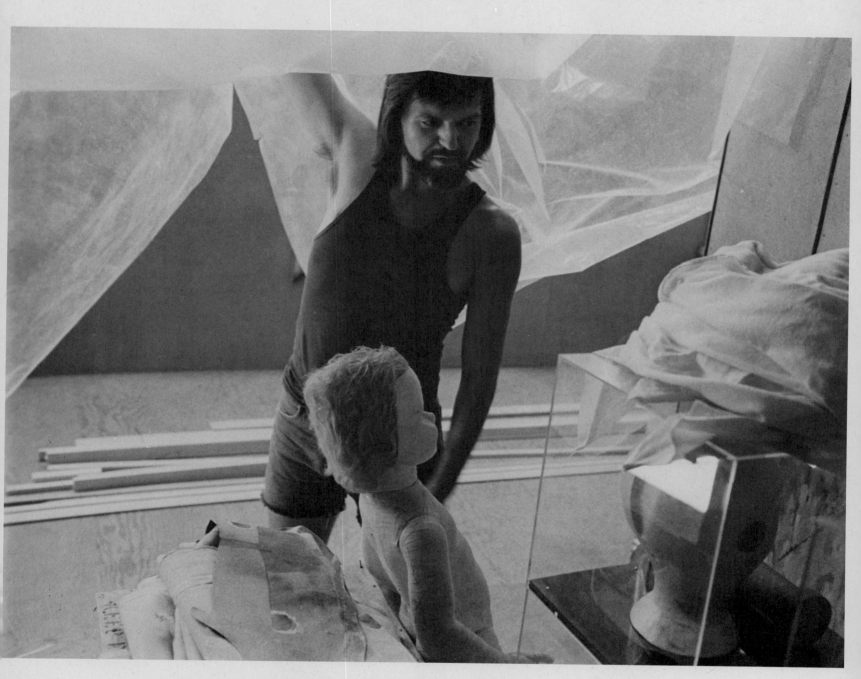

I prefer any statement I have made visually to any that I could write.

A concerted look at Canadian war art makes it clear that war, like most things, has an almost pastoral quality for many Canadian painters. In contrast to the war art of other countries, that produced by Canadian artists has (with notable exceptions) missed the point. "War is heck" seems to be their motto: they choose to ignore its horrors and prefer instead to concentrate on the quaint villages of France or the abstract patterns formed by rows of camouflaged trucks.

This uncritical serenity is an established part of Canadian art as a whole; our leading artists have, for some reason, traditionally shied away from social commentary; for years our galleries have been hung with mile after mile of bland, tasteful landscapes, a few pleasant portraits, and even fewer anecdotal paintings, all refined and in good taste. What has been largely missing is any gutsy sense of the pain or ugliness that is some part of life.

Claude Breeze is a distinct exception to the genteel mainstream; his paintings pulsate with the agony of existence seen against an erotic counterpoint.

The art production of the period under discussion is mainly abstract, where there is no "subject" as such; without a discernible "subject," of course, there can be little direct social commentary in works of art. But there have been a number of highly professional Canadian artists who have resisted the twentieth-century abstract "academy" and who pursued the less fashionable route of figurative art (among them Colville and Chambers, pages 57-64 and 129-36). But Breeze is not just a figurative artist; his paintings are thick with content, feeling and social commentary. His work is uniquely un-Canadian in the way it always expresses an editorial position that is often disturbingly provocative and, until recently, almost always violent.

The violence of Breeze's imagery and the nature of his subject matter come from a very personal view of the world; there is nothing in either his background or in the work of his teachers to explain it. He was born in Nelson, B.C. in 1938 and educated at the Regina School of Art at the University of Saskatchewan. It's hard to believe that he shared with his close friend, Brian Fisher (pages 201-8), the same group of distinguished teachers: Art MacKay, Roy Kiyooka (pages 89-96) and Ron Bloore (pages 81-8). He studied as well under the much-respected "magic realist of the west," Ernest Lindner, but Lindner's gentle studies of nature give no clue to Breeze's strident, journalistic realism.

Ron Bloore remembers him as a belligerent, truculent student, aggressively fighting to maintain his individuality and quarrelling with the school curriculum. Nonetheless, he graduated with a B grade. Despite his battles, Breeze seems to have suffered through the derivative stage common to most young artists. His principal influence for some time was the English expressionist painter Francis Bacon, as *Hopscotch* (ill. p. 197) makes clear.

After graduating from the Regina School of Art in 1958, Breeze spent a year at the Vancouver School of Art, and settled in downtown Vancouver. By the early sixties, he was beginning to develop his own style, more especially exercising his own unique choice of subject material, as in *Sunday Afternoon: From an Old American Photograph* (ill. p. 199). Its form stems from German expressionism, which has been only a minor influence on Canadian painting, although it has had adherents in the faculty of the Ontario College of Art and elsewhere, among artists scattered across the country, including the strongly influential Western painter, Maxwell Bates.

Breeze's strength has been his ability to bring together the German expressionist style and a subject matter which is particularly suited to that style. In the beginning, his ability to combine the two was less sure than it is now; the figures of his paintings were out of harmony with the background. Breeze considers his *Hill Raja's Dream* pivotal to his work; in it he himself began to see the difficulties of the road he had chosen.

Like the background to *Sunday Afternoon, Hill Raja's Dream* shows the influence exerted on Breeze by Persian miniature painting; the all-over patterns evident in his work, as well as the Oriental rendering of space in which objects at a distance are not seen in Western-style perspective but are placed above those which are closer. Some of the tension of Breeze's work comes not just from its themes of sex and violence but from the uneasy mix between German expressionist, pop art colouring, and Oriental space. By the time Breeze completed his *Lovers in a Landscape* series, he had fully mastered the problems of integrating form and content; one of this series (ill. p. 198), was painted in 1965 and is now in the Art Gallery of Ontario collection.

In about the same period Breeze became interested in pop art and particularly in the work of de Kooning; Breeze, while working on *Lovers in a Landscape*, was also doing another group, *Ruby Red Lips Blue Eyed Baby* which, though not pop art in style, was decidedly pop art in content. It is important to keep in mind that Breeze, while influenced by a variety of other kinds of painting, still brings to his work his own highly individual approach and talent.

By the mid-sixties his work was being accepted in exhibitions outside Vancouver, beginning with the National Gallery Biennial of 1965; in 1967 he burst upon the Toronto scene with a one-man show at the Jerrold Morris Gallery, was included in the *Perspective '67* show at the Art Gallery of Ontario, the Canadian Group of Painters exhibit in Montreal and, finally, won the first purchase award in *British Columbia '67* at the Vancouver Art Gallery. By the end of the centennial year, Breeze was established as an artist of national stature.

The following year, Breeze came to international attention in an exhibition, *West Coast Now*, shown in both Los Angeles and San Francisco; he was also represented at the Edinburgh Festival in the exhibit *Canada 101*, and at an exhibition in Chicago dealing with civil liberties. In that same year his work was first purchased by the Canada Council for its own collection.

Claude Breeze is a muscular, stocky, highly physical man who has always lived in the casual, outdoors manner of the West Coast. In 1969, Breeze moved to the Vancouver suburb of North Surrey which, though only a half hour's drive from downtown, is situated in a lush rain forest. His home is cottage-like, using the local materials and overlooking a spectacular view. Much of the house is wood, emphasizing its relationship to the forest in which it nestles. For a period, Breeze worked as a medical artist and his experience drawing from cadavers may account for his eerie treatment of the human figure, with its particular emphasis on body parts. He now supplements his income from the sale of his work by doing a little teaching when, in his words, "I need the bread."

In the year of his first great national prominence, 1967, Breeze solved the pictorial problem which had been evident in his work till that time, a problem as old as art itself; the relationship of figures to their background so that they meld into a whole. Even some of the Renaissance masters had difficulty making the people in their compositions appear as natural, integrated elements in the environment, rather than cut-outs pasted onto the surface of a painted backdrop. In a series, *The Home Viewer*, Breeze used the familiar shape of the TV screen as a framing device in which the figures and background were fused into one indivisible whole.

In 1968, Breeze had spent the summer painting in the area of Horseshoe Bay, northwest of Vancouver, using shaped canvases and a spray gun for the first time. The result was a new series he called *Island*; the experience probably was one factor in his decision to move to North Surrey.

For a year after arriving there, Breeze devoted much of his time to renovating the old cottage in which he now lives and he produced no paintings in that time. Once he started again, his paintings showed, in the words of Barry Lord's article in the August-September 1971 *artscanada*,". . . [Breeze's] growing awareness of the landscape around him."

Claude Breeze has been secretive about his most recent art, which is said to be lyrical and less violent than in the past, and his right to privacy, while he works through these new changes, whatever they are, must be respected; in keeping with this need, Breeze has decided not to make a verbal statement.

Whatever the nature of his most recent work, on the basis of his past performance one can be sure that he will continue to be a "high risk" artist, willing to chance his recognizable image in an effort to expand and improve his expressive means. Using these means, Breeze has said a great deal about man's relationship to his fellows and to his environment, statements which are at one and the same time profound and universal.

196

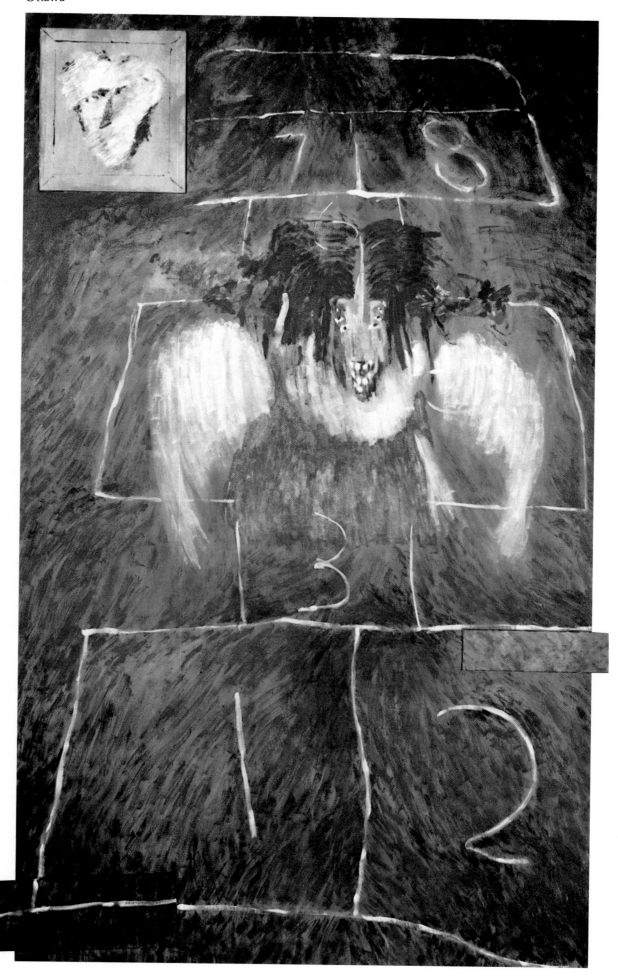

Claude Breeze
Lovers in the Landscape (No. 6)
acrylic on canvas
70″ x 70″   1965
Art Galley of Ontario
(Gift from Anonymous Fund &
Canada Council Matching Grant, 1965),
Toronto

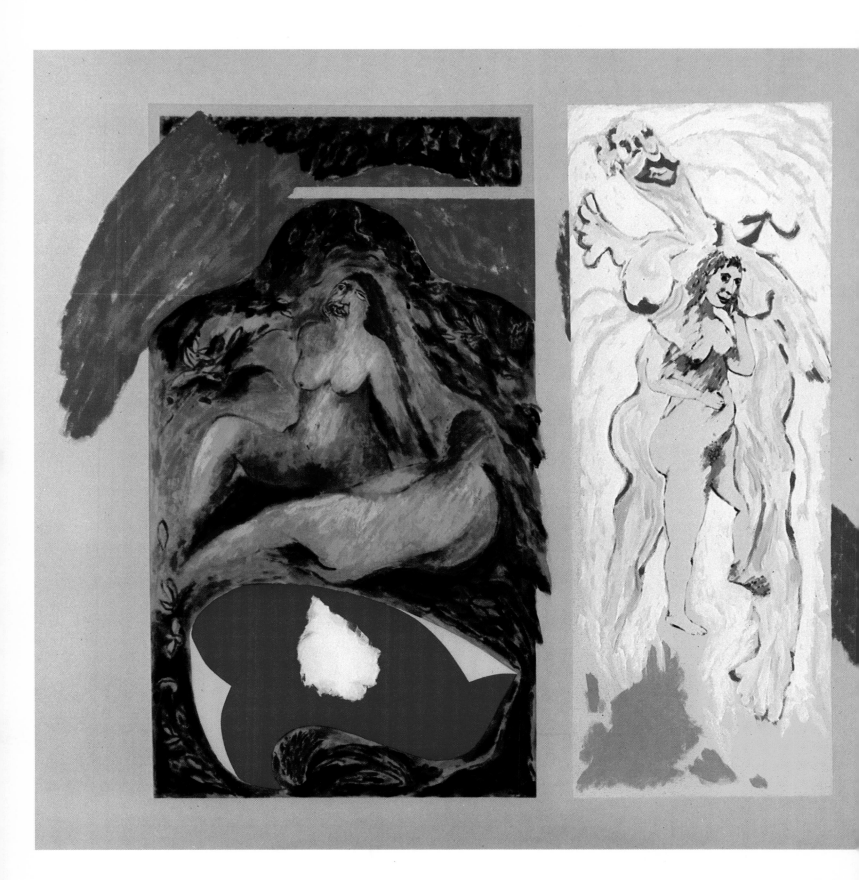

Claude Breeze
Transmission Difficulties: The Operation
acrylic on canvas
68'' x 94''   1968
National Gallery of Canada,
Ottawa

Brian Fisher

I have become wary of making statements about art in general and my own work in particular, since previous half-baked pronouncements keep coming back to haunt me. Better to shut up and listen to the poets.

William Carlos Williams says it in his poem "Tribute to the Painters" ...
*   The Dream*
*   is in pursuit!*

Perhaps one measure of the growing acceptance (if not always the perceived importance) of art in Canadian life is the contrast between the careers of Jock Macdonald, the first artist in this book, and Brian Fisher, with whom it closes.

We see Macdonald in isolation, virtually unknown and unshown (except in the Painters Eleven exhibits which came later in his life), passing on to several generations of students what he had painstakingly learned himself. His training was European and, like the artists of his generation, he looked there, then to New York, for his initial inspiration. He was a man past his sixtieth birthday, in the last year of his life, before he was accorded his first major one man show, and he died without ever having received a commission for his work.

In contrast, Brian Fisher, born forty-two years after Macdonald, was exhibiting while still in his mid-twenties; within three years he had appeared in two major Canadian shows, in an important international exhibit, and had been awarded a prestigious commission by the Canadian Government while would-be buyers waited patiently to purchase his work. His schooling has been largely Canadian and his artistic concerns are not in Paris or New York, but in a style of art without specific national boundaries or locale.

Brian Fisher is a fine draftsman and technician who has complete mastery of his art, a man who creates works that have great depth beyond their sensual surface. In the same way that the solution to a complex mathematical problem has connotations of beauty, the intricacy of Fisher's work fascinates the viewer. Not surprisingly, he is himself interested in avant-garde theories in both mathematics and sciences, as well as in Zen and the occult.

David Thompson, writing in the catalogue of the Canada Council Collection travelling exhibit in 1969, says, "Brian Fisher . . . is one of those West Coast painters whose work seems to look across to the far side of the Pacific in its serenity . . . in black and white his meticulous distinction of style achieves effects of considerable, aristocratic power."

All of the prairie painters acknowledge the profound influence of the great space of the flatland on their work and Fisher is no exception. Born in Uxbridge, England, of Canadian parents, he was brought to this country when only a year old and spent the next nineteen years in Regina. From 1957 to 1959 he attended Regina College, followed by the School of Art at the University of Saskatchewan and then the Vancouver School of Art.

At the University of Saskatchewan he had several notable teachers: Roy Kiyooka (pages 89-96), Art McKay, Ron Bloore (pages 81-8) and Ken Lochhead (pages 97-104) among them; exposure to this group makes him a member of the second generation of Regina painters.

In 1962, Fisher went to Europe to study on a Canada Council grant and was able to stay on by winning an Italian Government scholarship for studies at the Accademia di Belle Arti in Rome. In 1964 he returned to Canada and took up residence in Vancouver, where he now lives.

Thoughtful and articulate, Fisher has examined the ideas of the men who have influenced him — principally his teachers — and has extrapolated from them elements which he has combined and manipulated so that they have become an integrated whole, specifically his.

His central focal image seems to have its roots in the work of Art McKay, who for many years was preoccupied with a central, circular motif. He was also strongly influenced by the formal, purist abstract paintings of his teacher Ron Bloore. Although their surface styles seem to have relatively little in common, the underlying structure of Fisher's work is evocative of Roy Kiyooka's elliptical forms and cool, precise colours. Fisher's interest in Zen was first awakened by Kiyooka and may explain a soaring other-worldly quality in his work.

Fisher's art is created in the style of traditional constructivism, descended from the constructions, made in the early years of this century, by a group of Europeans, including Antoine Pesvner and Naum Gabo; they were part of a school who, rather than artistically rejecting the industrial age, used its materials and techniques in their work.

Fisher's paintings explore the concept of space and its effect, both intellectual and emotional, on human beings. They have been classified as op art because of the vibrations that are often set up on the retina of the eye, a result of the fine web-work of interlacing lines on the canvas. His images, which are built up from many small components, often appear to fluctuate between unity and diversity; they assume different aspects depending on the distance or angle from which they are viewed. From far away they may appear to be calm and peaceful, but at close quarters they vibrate with an almost electronic intensity. His intention, however, is to go beyond optical gymnastics: it is our relation to space, especially landscape space, that forms the "subject matter" of Fisher's work.

In approaching Fisher's art, viewers have to be aware that looking is not seeing: there are two levels involved and these two are somewhat related to the amount of time the spectator is prepared to spend with each painting achieved. The first impression is of sensual delight; the second, only after more focused attention, is serene and contemplative. Fisher suggests at least a half-hour's concentration on each canvas in order to penetrate the superficial visual pleasure, beyond which lies the Zen-like experience of total understanding.

Brian Fisher lives in a large frame house, an example of the older wooden Vancouver dwellings; his studio is at the back of the yard, in a separate building. Like John Meredith, he pours his life into his work, eschewing the art association and teaching. A waiting list of prospective buyers has, for some time, purchased his work even before it was completed. A fresh-faced man of medium build, he is quietly sociable and has an engaging sense of humour; when not painting he putters around his house or writes poetry. The artist takes the intellectual basis for his work very seriously and talks about it with great conviction and clarity: in speaking of the various tensions in his compositions he says, "The human preference for symmetry and order has given way to the recognition that order and disorder must be accepted on an equal basis." Of his continued preoccupation with the constructivist image he says, "Definition of structure itself has become the subject," a remark closely allied to the McLuhan "medium-is-the-message" concept.

Brian Fisher first came to national attention when he was included in the Canadian Pavilion at Expo '67 in Montreal in the same year he was chosen by the English artist and teacher Richard Hamilton for the painting section of *Perspective '67*, the Canadian Centennial exhibition at the Art Gallery of Ontario. The following year, he was selected as one of the artists who represented this country in the Edinburgh Festival Show, *Canada 101*. In the late sixties, Fisher received three important commissions: a banner for the Confederation Centre in Charlottetown, P.E.I., a Canadian United Nations Commemorative postage stamp, and a mural for the Montreal International Airport at Dorval (ill. p. 207). The latter has been called "one of the most successful marriages of art and architecture in Canada." His work is now in the collection of every major art museum and university in Canada.

Fisher's most recent work gives way to a more static, simpler structure: speaking of *Steppes*, a series (ill. p. 208), he says, "The space where all these lines are converging is what is known. The lines are positive in the sense that they can be measured, graphed, and so on. The space on the other side of them is what is not known. If one is going to offer encouragement to take a step off a cliff, one should give a feeling that there's a net below. The blue is very comfortable and lacking in anxiety somehow. It's a question of being able to operate easily in the totally unknown."

"Unknown" is the key: art is an exploration of that which is still unfamiliar territory to most of us. Artists, whether in Macdonald's later free and poetic style or in the cerebral and disciplined webs of Brian Fisher, are our guides in that world which lies beyond our everyday existence.

Brian Fisher
Enigma
polymer acrylic on cotton canvas
68'' x 68''   1966
Queen's University,
Kingston

Brian Fisher
Transfixion
acrylic on canvas
56″ x 68″   1966
Department of External Affairs,
Ottawa

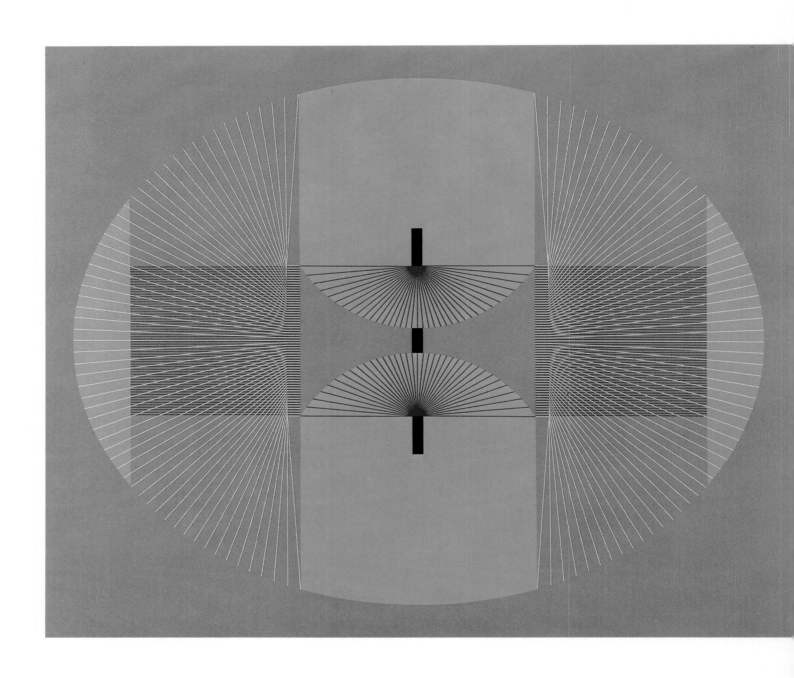

Brian Fisher
Night Flight (mural)
polymer acrylic on fibreglass panels
120'' x 288''   1968
Department of Transport,
Montreal

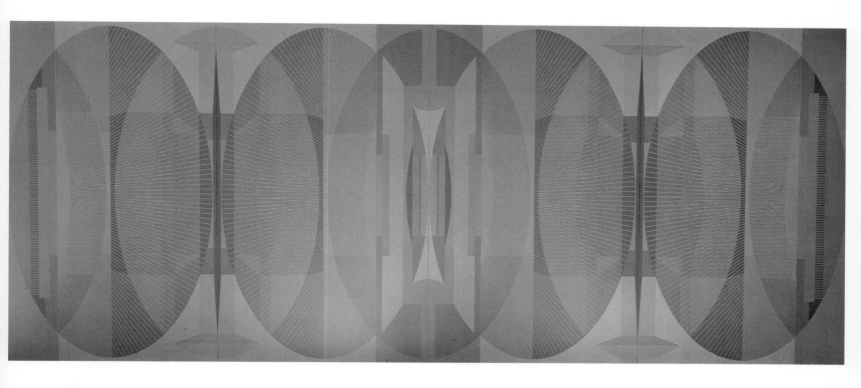

Brian Fisher
Steppe II No. 3
polymer acrylic on canvas
66″ x 132″   1970
National Gallery of Canada,
Ottawa

No attempt has been made to record everything which has been published on the artists discussed. The titles of books, catalogues of exhibitions, and articles listed are those which provide useful information for the general reader. The emphasis is on critical comment and therefore picture books and catalogues of exhibitions containing a minimum of text have been omitted.

GENERAL

D. W. Buchanan, *The Growth of Canadian Painting*, Toronto, Collins, 1950.

J. R. Harper, *Painting in Canada, a History,* Toronto, University of Toronto Press, 1966.

R. H. Hubbard, *The Development of Canadian Art*, Ottawa, National Gallery of Canada, 1963.

Colin S. Macdonald, *A Dictionary of Canadian Artists*, Ottawa, Canadian Paperbacks, 1967.

Guy Viau, *La Peinture Moderne au Canada Français*, Québec, Ministère des Affaires Culturelles, 1964.

RONALD BLOORE

Collections include: Art Gallery of Ontario; London (Ontario) Art Gallery; National Gallery of Canada; New Brunswick Art Gallery, Saint John; Confederation Art Gallery, Charlottetown; Dorval Airport, Montreal; York University; Musée d'Art Contemporain; Montreal Museum of Fine Arts; The Mendel Gallery, Saskatoon; Winnipeg Art Gallery; Vancouver Art Gallery; Agnes Etherington Art Centre, Kingston; Art Gallery of Greater Victoria; Simon Fraser University; Beaverbrook Art Gallery.

R. B. Simmins, "R. L. Bloore", *Canadian Art,* v. 19 (March/April 1962), 114-115, 154.

D. P. Silcox, "Ronald Bloore at the Here and Now Gallery, Toronto", *Canadian Art,* v. 19 (May/June 1962), 176.

Barry Lord, "Ronald Bloore and Contemporary Art Criticism", *Canadian Art,* v. 23 (Oct. 1966), 22-24.

Barry Lord, "Ronald Bloore [at] the Jerrold Morris Gallery", *artscanada,* v. 26 (Feb. 1969), 39-40.

Barry Lord, "White/Light; a Visit to Ronald Bloore and his New Paintings", *artscanada,* v. 27 (Feb. 1970), 15-23.

PAUL-EMILE BORDUAS

Collections include: Montreal Museum of Fine Arts; Musée de la Province
de Québec; National Gallery of Canada; Museum of Modern Art; Art Gallery
of Ontario.

Robert Elie, *Borduas*, Montréal, L'Arbre, 1943.
D. G. Seckler, "Paul-Emile Borduas", *Arts*, v. 29 (June 1, 1955), 8-10.
Robert Elie and Jean Ethier-Blais, "Hommage à Paul-Emile Borduas",
    Vie des Arts, no. 19 (Summer 1960), 18-31.
Montreal Museum of Fine Arts, *Paul-Emile Borduas 1905-1960 [Exhibition*
    Catalogue. Preface by Evan H. Turner], 1962.
"Borduas Inédit", *Liberté*, v. 4 (Jan.-Feb. 1962), 3-20. (Contains "Une Vie de
    Peintre", by Jacques Folch; "Borduas Parle" [radio interviews];
    "Témoinage" by Robert Elie; "Notes sur Borduas" by André Jasmin.)
"Documents [on] Borduas", *Liberté*, v. 4 (April 1962), 225-263. (Contains
    "Dimensions de Borduas" by Claude Gauvreau; "Lettres à Claude Gauvreau"
    from Borduas; "Epilogue et Méditation" by Jean Ethier-Blais.)
Musée d'Art Contemporain, Montreal, *Borduas et les Automatistes, Montréal*
    1942-1955 [Texts by Bernard Teyssèdre, Fernand Dumont and others], 1971.
    (Includes "Le Refus Global".)

CLAUDE BREEZE

Collections include: Vancouver Art Gallery; Art Gallery of Ontario;
New Brunswick Museum; Queen's University; University of British Columbia;
Mount Allison University; York University; University of Western Ontario;
Art Gallery of Greater Victoria; London (Ontario) Art Gallery; Brantford
Art Gallery; The Mendel Gallery, Saskatoon.

Barry Lord, "Sunday Afternoon", *artscanada*, v. 24 (Jan. 1967), 13-16.
R. B. Simmins, "Claude Breeze: Recent Paintings and Drawings, Bau-Xi
    Gallery, November", *artscanada*, v. 26 (Feb. 1969), 37.
Barry Lord, "Breeze in Retrospect [at] University of Waterloo January 1969",
    artscanada, v. 26 (April 1969), 36-37.
Joan Lowndes, "Claude Breeze: Drawings Bau-Xi Gallery, Vancouver,
    November 1970", *artscanada*, v. 28 (Feb./March 1971), 48-49.
Barry Lord, "From the 'Deck' at North Surrey: Landscape and Figure in the
    Art of Claude Breeze", *artscanada*, v. 28 (Aug./Sept. 1971), 28-36.

ALEX COLVILLE

Collections include: National Gallery of Canada; Art Gallery of Ontario; Montreal Museum of Fine Arts; Art Gallery of Hamilton; Museum of Modern Art; Wallraf-Richarts Museum, Cologne; Kestner Geselleschaft, Hanover; Centre Nationale d'Art Contemporaine.

Avery Shaw, "Towards a Personal Realism", *Canadian Art*, v. 8 (Summer 1951), 162-164.

Lincoln Kirstein, "Alex Colville", *Canadian Art*, v. 15 (August 1958), 216-219.

H. J. Dow, "Magic Realism of Alex Colville", *Art Journal*, v. 24 (Summer 1965), 318-329).

P. Æ. Hutchings, "Realism, Surrealism and Celebration: the Paintings of Alex Colville in the Collection of the National Gallery of Canada", *National Gallery of Canada*, Bulletin No. 8 (1966), 16-28.

Marlborough Fine Art Ltd., London, *Alex Colville [Exhibition Catalogue. Text by Robert Melville]*, 1970.

H. J. Dow, "Alex Colville, a Modern Poussin", *Journal of Canadian Studies*, Trent University, v. 6 (Nov. 1971), 54-62.

GREG CURNOE

Collections include: National Gallery of Canada; University of British Columbia; Vancouver Art Gallery; Norman Mackenzie Art Gallery, Regina; Montreal Museum of Fine Arts; Art Gallery of Ontario; University of Western Ontario; London (Ontario) Art Gallery.

Laura Stewart, comp., "Who's Who in Ontario Art: Greg Curnoe [bio-bibliography]", *Ontario Library Review*, v. 50 (Dec. 1966), 274-276.

J. N. Chandler, "More Words on Curnoe's Wordy World", *artscanada*, v. 26 (April 1969), 3-8.

National Gallery of Canada, Ottawa, *Greg Curnoe, Canada. [Exhibition at the] X Biennial, Saõ Paulo, 1969. Catalogue by Dennis Reid. Exhibition Organized by the National Gallery of Canada, Ottawa.* Ottawa, Published by the National Gallery of Canada for the Queen's Printer, 1969.

Barrie Hale, "Stick around and Work with What's Around You", *Saturday Night*, Toronto, v. 85 (Jan. 1970), 25-29.

J. N. Chandler, "Painting from Life", *artscanada*, v. 28 (June/July 1971), 75-76.

BRIAN FISHER

Collections include: Montreal Museum of Fine Arts; Memorial University Art Gallery; Vancouver Art Gallery; University of Western Ontario;

Art Gallery of Greater Victoria; Art Gallery of Ontario; Norman Mackenzie
Art Gallery, Regina; University of Alberta; Willistead Art Gallery, Windsor;
University of British Columbia; Edmonton Art Gallery; University of Victoria;
York University; Confederation Art Gallery, Charlottetown; Queen's
University; National Gallery of Canada.

Norman Mackenzie Art Gallery, Regina, Sask., *Contrasts: Brian Fisher* [*and*]
    Claude Breeze [*Exhibition Catalogue. Text by Terry Fenton*], 1967.
Philip Leider, "Vancouver: Scene with no Scene", *artscanada*, v. 24 (June/July,
    1967), 8.
Joan Lowndes, "The Odyssey of Brian Fisher", *Vancouver Province*,
    March 7, 1969, 12.

YVES GAUCHER

Collections include: Museum of Modern Art; Victoria and Albert Museum;
National Gallery of Canada; Art Gallery of Ontario; Montreal Museum of
Fine Arts; Musée de la Province de Québec; Musée d'Art Contemporain;
Vancouver Art Gallery; Winnipeg Art Gallery; Willistead Art Gallery,
Windsor; Sir George Williams University; Queen's University; York
University; University of British Columbia; Hart House Collection;
University of Western Ontario; Confederation Art Gallery, Charlottetown;
Edmonton Art Gallery; University of Moncton; Regina Public Library;
Art Institute of Ontario; Musée de Québec.

M. E. Cutler, "Artist in Perspective: Yves Gaucher Interviewed", *Canadian Art,*
    v. 22 (Sept./Oct. 1965), 26-28.
Jacques Folch, "Yves Gaucher", *Vie des Arts*, no. 41 (Winter 1965/66), 40-43,
    (English summary) 52.
Anne Brodzky, "Notice also Silent Sounds; the New Work of Yves Gaucher",
    Artscanada, v. 25 (June 1968), 21-23.
Vancouver Art Gallery, *Yves Gaucher* [*Exhibition Catalogue. Text by
    Doris Shadbolt*], 1969.
David Silcox, "Yves Gaucher", *Studio International*, v. 177 (Feb. 1969), 76-77.

TED GODWIN

Collections include: National Gallery of Canada; Art Gallery of Ontario;
Beaverbrook Art Gallery; Norman Mackenzie Art Gallery, Regina;
Agnes Etherington Art Centre, Kingston; University of Manitoba;
University of Calgary; Guelph Agricultural College.

R. B. Simmins, "Godwin", *Canadian Art*, v. 19 (March/April 1962), 124-125.

Ontario Library Association, Reference Workshop Committee, "Who's Who in Ontario Art, pt. 8: James Williamson Galloway Macdonald [bio-bibliography]", *Ontario Library Review,* v. 33 (August 1949), 257-258.

Maxwell Bates, "Jock Macdonald Painter-Explorer", *Canadian Art,* v. 14 (Summer 1957), 151-153.

Paul Duval, "Jock Macdonald at the Roberts Gallery, Toronto", *Canadian Art,* v. 19 (March/April 1962), 107.

M. E. Cutler, "Borduas and Macdonald: Canada's Greatest Art Teachers", *Canadian Art,* v. 22 (Nov./Dec. 1965), 21.

National Gallery of Canada, Ottawa, *Jock Macdonald, Retrospective Exhibition. Exhibition and Catalogue by R. Ann Pollock [and] Dennis R. Reid,* 1969.

JOHN MEREDITH

Collections include: Art Gallery of Ontario; Museum of Modern Art; National Gallery of Canada; Montreal Museum of Fine Arts; University of Waterloo; Norman Mackenzie Art Gallery, Regina; Vancouver Art Gallery; Willistead Art Gallery, Windsor; Agnes Etherington Art Centre, Kingston; Confederation Art Gallery, Charlottetown.

Barry Lord, "John Meredith at the Isaacs Gallery", *artscanada,* v. 24 (March 1967, supp.), 4.

Barry Lord, "John Meredith, Painter", *artscanada,* v. 26 (April 1969), 16-22.

Barry Lord, "John Meredith: the Isaacs Gallery, Toronto", *artscanada,* v. 27 (Feb. 1970), 52.

Barrie Hale, "Canada: Recent Exhibitions", *Arts Magazine,* v. 44 (Feb. 1970), 52.

GUIDO MOLINARI

Collections include: Museum of Modern Art; Guggenheim Museum; Vancouver Art Gallery; Edmonton Art Gallery; Norman Mackenzie Art Gallery, Regina; Winnipeg Art Gallery; Art Gallery of Ontario; National Gallery of Canada; Montreal Museum of Fine Arts; Musée d'Art Contemporain; Sir George Williams University; York University; Carleton University; Hart House Collection.

Vancouver Art Gallery, *Molinari [Catalogue of an Exhibition],* 1964.

Fernande Saint-Martin, "Le Dynamisme des Plasticiens de Montréal", *Vie des Arts,* no. 44 (Autumn 1966), 44-45, (English summary) 98.

Venice. Biennial Exhibition, 1968 (34th), Canada. *Ulysse Comtois/ Guido Molinari.* [*Catalogue of an Exhibition*] *Organized by the National Gallery of Canada, Ottawa.* [*Introduction by Brydon Smith and Pierre Théberge*], Ottawa, Queen's Printer, 1968.

Barry Lord, "New Work from Montreal", *Art in America,* v. 57 (May/June 1969), 101.

Pierre Théberge, "Molinari, an Interview, *artscanada,* v. 26 (June 1969), 37-38.

Guido Molinari, "L'Ecrivain a des Antennes", *Liberté,* v. 11 (Mai-Juillet), 115-119.

ALFRED PELLAN

Collections include: Quebec Provincial Museum; National Gallery of Canada; Montreal Museum of Fine Arts; Art Gallery of Ontario; Beaverbrook Art Gallery; Art Gallery of Hamilton; Art Gallery of Edmonton; Kitchener-Waterloo Art Gallery; Dalhousie Art Gallery; Le Musée d'Art Contemporain; Willistead Art Gallery, Windsor; Norman Mackenzie Art Gallery, Regina.

Maurice Gagnon, *Pellan,* Montréal, L'Arbre, 1943. (Collection Art Vivant.)

Joe Plaskett, "Paris Honours Alfred Pellan", *Canadian Art,* v. 12 (Spring 1955), 113-115.

National Gallery of Canada, Ottawa, *Alfred Pellan* [*Catalogue of a Retrospective Exhibition*] *The National Gallery of Canada, The Montreal Museum of Fine Arts, Le Musée de la Province de Quebéc, The Art Gallery of Toronto.* [*Introduction by D. W. Buchanan. Mes Tableaux ce sont Mes Inquiétudes, par Paul Gladu.*], Ottawa, Queen's Printer, 1960.

D. W. Buchanan, *Alfred Pellan,* Toronto, Society for Art Publications/ McClelland and Stewart, 1962.

Guy Robert, *Pellan: Sa Vie et Son Oeuvre. His Life and His Art,* Montréal, Editions du Centre de Psychologie et de Pédagogie [1963]. (Collection Artistes Canadiens.)

Alfred Pellan, "Pellan Parle [une Entrevue par Jacques Folch]", *Liberté,* v. 9 (March/April 1967), 64-69.

Henri Barras, "Un Cinéaste Face à un Artiste" [Review of film "Voir Pellan" produced by Louis Portugais], *Culture Vivante,* Québec, no. 13 (May 1969), 32-37.

Musée du Québec, Québec, "Alfred Pellan: Special Issue including Autobiographical Notes and Comments Recorded in an Interview, by André Marchand", Its *Bulletin,* no. 14 (March 1970), 1-5.

GORDON RAYNER

Collections include: National Gallery of Canada; Art Gallery of Ontario; Vancouver Art Gallery; Montreal Museum of Fine Arts; University of Waterloo; Museum of Modern Art; Willistead Art Gallery, Windsor; Agnes Etherington Art Centre, Kingston; Confederation Art Gallery, Charlottetown; Norman Mackenzie Art Gallery, Regina; Winnipeg Art Gallery.

Robert Markle, "Gordon Rayner [at] the Isaacs Gallery", *artscanada*, v. 26 (June 1969), 47-48.
Barrie Hale, "Gordon Rayner: the First Decade", *artscanada*, v. 27 (Feb. 1970), 24-29.

JEAN-PAUL RIOPELLE

Collections include: National Gallery of Canada; Museum of Modern Art; Musée d'Art Moderne, Paris; Tate Gallery; Agnes Etherington Art Centre, Kingston; Musée de Québec.

Pierre Schneider, "Jean-Paul Riopelle", *L'Oeil*, no. 18 (June 1956), 36-41, 47.
Patrick Heron, "Riopelle and the Controlled Accident", *Arts*, v. 30 (June 1956), 12.
Frank O'Hara, "Riopelle: International Speedscapes", *Art News*, v. 62 (April 1963), 32-34, 64-65.
Musée du Québec, Québec, *Riopelle* [*Exhibition Catalogue. Text by Pierre Schneider*], 1967.
Guy Robert, *Riopelle: ou, La Poétique du Geste*, Montréal, Editions de l'Homme, 1970.
Michael Greenwood, "Jean-Paul Riopelle: Poet of the Sign", *artscanada*, v. 28 (Aug./Sept. 1971), 66-68.

WILLIAM RONALD

Collections include: Art Gallery of Ontario; Guggenheim Museum; Museum of Modern Art; National Gallery of Canada; Allbright-Knox Art Gallery, Buffalo; University of British Columbia; Montreal Museum of Fine Arts; Agnes Etherington Art Centre, Kingston; Whitney Museum of Art; Robert McLaughlin Gallery, Oshawa; York University.

I. S., "William Ronald [at the Kootz Gallery]", *Art News*, v. 56 (April 1957), 14.
David Ralston and Hugo McPherson, "The Ronald Chapel in Toronto Harbour", *Canadian Art*, v. 23 (April 1966), 28-31.
William Cameron, "Portrait of the Artist as a Violently Honest Man", *Maclean's*, v. 84 (Feb. 1971), 33-37.

JACK SHADBOLT

Collections include: National Gallery of Canada; Art Gallery of Ontario;
Simon Fraser University; University of British Columbia; Fathers of
Confederation Gallery, Charlottetown; McMaster University; Sarnia Public
Library and Art Gallery; Saskatoon Gallery and Conservatory Confederation;
University of Manitoba School of Art; Vancouver Art Gallery.

D. W. Buchanan, "Shadbolt Explores a World of Roots and Seeds",
    Canadian Art, v. 8 (Spring 1951), 112-114.
Richard Lawrence, "The Man Who Paints Nightmares", *Mayfair*,
    (Dec. 1951), 57-59, 99-105.
Colin Graham, "A Year in the Sun", *Canadian Art*, v. 15 (April 1958),
    94-97, 148-149.
Jack Shadbolt, *In Search of Form*, Toronto, McClelland and Stewart, 1968.
National Gallery of Canada, Ottawa, *Jack Shadbolt [Catalogue of an]*
    Exhibition Organized by the Vancouver Art Gallery and Circulated by the
    National Gallery of Canada. [Introduction by Anthony M. Emery.
    Statements by the Artist.], Ottawa, Published by the National Gallery of
    Canada for the Queen's Printer, 1969.]
Marguerite Pinney, "Jack Shadbolt: the Bau-Xi Gallery", *artscanada,*
    v. 28 (April/May 1971), 81.

MICHAEL SNOW

Collections include: Museum of Modern Art; Vancouver Art Gallery;
National Gallery of Canada; Winnipeg Art Gallery; Art Gallery of Ontario;
Edmonton Art Gallery; Montreal Museum of Fine Arts; Norman Mackenzie
Art Gallery, Regina.

Arnold Rockman, "Michael Snow and his 'Walking Woman' ", *Canadian Art*,
    v. 20 (Nov./Dec. 1963), 345-347.
[Anne Brodzky, ed.], "7 Questions + 1 on Michael Snow at the Isaacs Gallery",
    artscanada, v. 26 (April 1969), 30-31.
Gene Youngblood, "Icon and Idea in the World of Michael Snow", *artscanada,*
    v. 27 (Feb. 1970), 2-14.
Art Gallery of Ontario, *Michael Snow: a Survey [Catalogue of an Exhibition]*
    Texts [by] Robert Fulford, Dennis Young, Richard Foreman [and]
    P. Adams Sitney. Book [Designed] by Michael Snow, Toronto, Published
    by the Art Gallery of Ontario in Collaboration with the Isaacs Gallery, 1970.
Richard Foreman, "Critique: Glass and Snow", *Arts Magazine*, v. 44
    (Feb. 1970), 20-22.

Venice. Biennial Exhibition, 1970 (35th), Canada. *Michael Snow [Catalogue of an Exhibition] Organized by the National Gallery of Canada, Ottawa. Commissioner for the Exhibition, Brydon Smith*, Ottawa, Published by the National Gallery of Canada for the Queen's Printer, 1970.

CLAUDE TOUSIGNANT

Collections include: National Gallery of Canada; Phoenix Museum; Larry Aldrich Museum; Montreal Museum of Fine Arts; Sir George Williams University; Museum of Fine Art; York University; Arts Council of Canada; Quebec Museum; Vancouver Art Gallery; Art Gallery of Ontario.

Fernande Saint-Martin, "Le Dynamisme des Plasticiens de Montréal: Claude Tousignant", *Vie des Arts,* no. 44 (Autumn 1966), 46, (English summary) 98.
Galerie du Siècle, Montréal, *Tousignant [Exhibition Catalogue. Text by Pierre Théberge]*, 1968, 4 pp.

HAROLD TOWN

Collections include: Museum of Modern Art; National Gallery of Canada; Stedelijk Museum; Art Gallery of Toronto; Montreal Museum of Fine Arts; Vancouver Art Gallery; Winnipeg Art Gallery; Beaverbrook Art Gallery; Edmonton Art Gallery; Art Gallery of Hamilton; London (Ontario) Art Gallery; Agnes Etherington Art Centre, Kingston; University of Guleph; Art Gallery of Oshawa; Hart House Collection; University of British Columbia; Norman Mackenzie Art Gallery, Regina; Kingston Art Society; Tate Gallery; Guggenheim Museum; Victoria Art Gallery; Mount Allison University; Sir George Williams University; University of Toronto; Willistead Art Gallery, Windsor; Metropolitan Museum of Art; York University; Musée d'Art Contemporain; Queen's University; Dalhousie University.

Ontario Library Association, Reference Workshop Committee, "Who's Who in Ontario Art, pt. 13: Harold Town [bio-bibliography]", *Ontario Library Review*, v. 35 (Feb. 1951), 81.
Barbara Moon, "The Overnight Bull Market in Modern Painting", *Maclean's*, v. 74 (Dec. 2, 1961), cover, 21-23, 38-41.
D. P. Silcox, "Harold Town at the Jerrold Morris Gallery, Toronto", *Canadian Art*, v. 19 (July/Aug. 1962), 259-260.

Alan Suddon and Laura Stewart, "Who's Who in Ontario Art: Harold Town
    [bio-bibliography]", *Ontario Library Review*, v. 48 (November 1964),
    216-221.
Harold Town, "To Canada with Love and Hisses", *Maclean's*, v. 78
    (Jan. 23, 1965), 13-15, 28-29, 32. (Includes the complete text of his
    "Enigmas".)
Harold Town, *Harold Town Drawings*, with an Introduction and Text by
    Robert Fulford, Toronto, McClelland and Stewart, 1969.
Barry Lord, "New Town Enigmas, Mazelow Gallery", *artscanada*,
    v. 26 (Aug. 1969), 39.
Michèle Tremblay, "Harold Town", *Vie des Arts*, no. 57 (Winter 1969/70), 63,
    (English translation) 82.
Robert Fulford, "Multiplicity of Harold Town", *artscanada,*
    v. 28 (April/May 1971), 49-58.

JOYCE WIELAND

Collections include: Vancouver Art Gallery; Art Gallery of Ontario;
National Gallery of Canada; University of Waterloo; Agnes Etherington
Art Centre, Kingston; Queen's University; Montreal Museum of Fine Arts;
Willistead Art Gallery, Windsor; Confederation Art Gallery, Charlottetown;
Winnipeg Art Gallery; Norman Mackenzie Art Gallery, Regina;
Edmonton Art Gallery; McMaster University; Museum of Modern Art.

David Donnell, "Joyce Wieland at the Isaacs Gallery, Toronto", *Canadian Art,*
    v. 21 (March/April 1964), 64.
Marguerite Pinney, "Joyce Wieland Retrospective, Vancouver Art Gallery",
    artscanada, v. 25 (June 1968), 41.
P. Adams Sitney, "There is only one Joyce", *artscanada*, v. 27
    (April 1970), 43-45.
Harry Malcolmson, " 'True Patriot Love' Joyce Wieland's New Show",
    Canadian Forum, v. 51 (June 1971), 17-18.
National Gallery of Canada, Ottawa, *True Patriot Love* [*Catalogue of an
    Exhibition*] *by Joyce Wieland.* [*The Film of Joyce Wieland by Regina
    Cornwell*] ... *Interview with Joyce Wieland, Interviewer, Pierre Théberge,*
    Ottawa, Published by the National Gallery of Canada for the Corporation
    of the National Museums of Canada, 1971.
Hugo McPherson, "Wieland: an Epiphany of North", *artscanada,* v. 28
    (Aug./Sept. 1971), 17-27.

Carmen Lamanna Gallery, 840 Yonge Street, Toronto
Galerie Dresdnere, 130 Bloor Street West, Toronto
Dunkelman Gallery, 15 Bedford Road, Toronto
Electric Gallery, 272 Avenue Road, Toronto
The Framing Gallery, 712 Bay Street, Toronto
The Innuit Gallery of Eskimo Art, 30 Avenue Road, Toronto
The Isaacs Gallery, 832 Yonge Street, Toronto
Laing Galleries, 194 Bloor Street West, Toronto
Marlborough Godard Gallery, 22 Hazelton Avenue, Toronto
Mazelow Gallery, 3463 Yonge Street, Toronto
David Mirvish Gallery, 596 Markham Street, Toronto
Gallery Moos, 138 Yorkville Avenue, Toronto
The Morris Gallery, 15 Prince Arthur, Toronto
Gallery Pascal, 104 Yorkville Avenue, Toronto
The Pollock Gallery, 356 Dundas Street West, Toronto
Roberts Gallery, 641 Yonge Street, Toronto
Albert White Gallery, 25 Prince Arthur, Toronto
Fleet Gallery, 173 McDermot Street East, Winnipeg
Continental Galleries Inc., 1450 Drummond St., Montreal
Dominion Gallery, 1438 Sherbrooke Street West, Montreal
Walter Klinkhoff Gallery, 1200 Sherbrooke Street West, Montreal
Galerie L'Art Français, 370 Laurier Avenue West, Montreal
Marlborough Godard Gallery, 1490 Sherbrooke Street West, Montreal
Galerie de Montréal, 2060 MacKay Street, Montreal
Lippel Gallery of Primitive Art, 2159 MacKay Street, Montreal
Waddington Galleries, 1456 Sherbrooke Street West, Montreal
Bau-Xi Gallery, 555 Hamilton Street, Vancouver
Beckett Gallery, 142 James Street South, Hamilton
Robertson Galleries, 162 Laurier Avenue West, Ottawa
Wells Gallery, 459 Sussex Drive, Ottawa
Galerie Zanettin, 28 Cote de la Montagne, Quebec
Zwicker's Gallery, 5415 Doyle Street, Halifax

THE ARTISTS

Ronald Bloore, *page 81*, Toronto *Star*
Paul-Emile Borduas, *page 25*, National Film Board of Canada
Claude Breeze, *page 193*, Tod Greenaway, Vancouver
Jack Bush, *page 49*, Villy Svarre, Toronto
Jack Chambers, *page 129,* John Reeves, Toronto
Alex Colville, *page 57*, Guido Mangold, Munich
Greg Curnoe, *page 185*, Bill McGrath, London, Ontario
Brian Fisher, *page 201*, Taki Blues Singer, Vancouver
Yves Gaucher, *page 169*, Charles Gagnon, Montreal
Ted Godwin, *page 153*, Yann Studios, Eire
Roy Kiyooka, *page 89*, Fred Douglas, Vancouver
Kenneth Lochhead, *page 97*, Ernie Mayer, Winnipeg
J. W. G. Macdonald, *page 17*, John Saxton, Toronto
John Meredith, *page 145*, John Reeves, Toronto
Guido Molinari, *page 161*, Robert Millet, Montreal
Alfred Pellan, *page 33*, Andre Le Coz, Montreal
Gordon Rayner, *page 177*, Toronto *Star*
Jean-Paul Riopelle, *page 65*, Jacques Dubourg, Paris
William Ronald, *page 105*, Art F. Oscar, Brandon, Manitoba
Jack Shadbolt, *page 41*, Ralph Bower, Vancouver *Sun*
Michael Snow, *page 113*, Amleto Lorenzini, Toronto
Claude Tousignant, *page 137*, Judith Terry, Montreal
Harold Town, *page 73*, John Reeves, Toronto
Joyce Wieland, *page 121*, Amleto Lorenzini, Toronto

Andre Emmerich Gallery, N.Y., *page 56*
Jean Pierre Beaudin, *page 87*
Ralph Bradatsch, *pages 158, 159, 160, 197*
The Clares, *page 64*
Dennis Colwell, *page 78*
Paul Duval, *page 175*
John Evans, *pages 24, 40, 93, 96, 149, 192, 199, 200, 205, 206, 208*
Julmar Graphics, *page 48*
A. Kilbertus, *pages 29, 141, 142, 143, 144, 176, 207*
Charles King, *pages 23, 32, 46, 61, 102*
Ian MacEachern, *page 190*
Otto Nelson, *page 31*
Eberhard Otto, *pages 88* (for *artscanada* magazine), *104* (for
    artscanada magazine), *133* (for *artscanada* magazine),
    134, 135, 136, 174
Jack Shadbolt, *page 47*
TDF Artists Limited, *page 71*
Ron Vickers, *pages 22, 38, 39, 45, 77, 79, 80, 85, 86, 95, 103, 110,
    111, 112, 119, 120, 125, 127, 128, 151, 152, 181, 182, 183, 184*
The Wallraf-Richartz Museum, *page 63*

Special thanks are due to the following galleries and
individuals who loaned colour transparencies:

Art Gallery of Ontario; National Gallery of Canada;
Nancy Poole's Studio, Toronto; York University, Toronto;
Andre Emmerich Gallery, New York; Confederation Art
Gallery and Museum; Stephan Hahn Gallery, New York;
Toronto-Dominion Bank; Marlborough/Godard
Gallery, Toronto; Schwendau Collection, London;
Alex Colville; Guido Molinari; Jean-Paul Riopelle.

JACKET DETAIL

This book was produced in Canada.

Typesetting: Mono Lino Typesetting Co. Limited
Film Separation: Herzig Somerville Limited
Printing: Ashton-Potter Limited
Binding: T. H. Best Printing Co. Limited